# THE IMAGE OF GOD THE FATHER

## IN ORTHODOX THEOLOGY
### AND
## ICONOGRAPHY
### AND
## OTHER STUDIES

D1453575

COVER: An image of God the Father as shown in the Patriarchal Church of Alexander Nevsky in Sofia, Bulgaria.
FRONTISPIECE: Design found in icons to represent God the Father.

# BY THE SAME AUTHOR

*Le lieu du coeur, Initiation à la spiritualité de l'Eglise orthodoxe*
Les Éditions du Cerf, Paris, 1989.

*Les chrétiens et les images*
Montréal, Québec, Éditions Paulines, 1992

*Etudes iconographiques*
Nethen, Belgium, Éditions Axios, 1993

# OTHER OFFERINGS FROM OAKWOOD

*The Icon: Image of the Invisible*
by Egon Sendler
Translated by Fr. Steven Bigham
1988

*Dynamic Symmetry Proportional System is Found in Some Byzantine & Russian Icons of the 14th to 16th Century*
by Karyl Knee
1988

*The Art of the Icon: a Theology of Beauty*
by Paul Evdokimov
Translated by Fr. Steven Bigham
1989

*The 'Painter's Manual' of Dionysius of Fourna*
ed. & trans. by Paul Hetherington
1990

*Icons & Iconpainting*
by Dennis Bell [VHS videotape]
1991

*Icon Collections*
by John Barns
1991

*The Ministry of Women in the Church*
by Elisabeth Behr-Sigel
Translated by Fr. Steven Bigham
1991

*An Iconographer's Patternbook: The Stroganov Tradition*
by Fr. Christopher Kelly
1992

*The Place of the Heart; An Introduction to Orthodox Sprituality*
by Elisabeth Behr-Sigel
Translated by Fr. Steven Bigham
1992

*The Illuminated Gospel of St. Matthew*
Original Calligraphy & Icons
by Vladislav Andrejev
1993

*Unknown Palekh*
by Vera Torzhkova
1993

*An Iconpainter's Notebook: The Bolshakov Edition*
Translated by Gregory Melnick
1994

*Orthodox Fathers, Orthodox Faith*
Touma Al-Khoury
1994

# THE IMAGE OF GOD THE FATHER

## IN ORTHODOX THEOLOGY
### AND
## ICONOGRAPHY
### AND
## OTHER STUDIES

# FR STEVEN BIGHAM

## DRAWINGS BY ALAIN VALLÉE

# Ωakwood IPublications

## TORRANCE, CALIFORNIA
## 1995

**ALL RIGHTS RESERVED**

# TABLE OF CONTENTS

# ILLUSTRATIONS

STUDIES IN ORTHODOX ICONOGRAPHY

# PREFACE

This publication is the fruit of over ten years of study and writing on a subject that fascinates, and haunts, that enigmatic creature called "modern man." What launched me on the path of iconographic studies was a course I took at St. Vladimir's Seminary in 1982 with Fr. Alexander Schmemann, about the Orthodox view of death as expressed in the Church's funeral rites. I decided to write on the way death and dead people are portrayed in icons. The paper I wrote received Fr. Alexander's approval – needless to say I was very pleased – and it appears here in English for the first time. Two other articles, on St. Gregory Palamas and St. Gregory Nyssa, are also the result of work done at the seminary. The text on Image of God the Father, with some revisions, is my M. Th. thesis. My interest in this particular subject resulted from a seemingly apparent contradiction, apparent at least to me: Church tradition clearly states that the Incarnation is the only basis on which a portrait of the invisible God can be painted, and yet "icons" of the Father and the Trinity abound in Orthodox Churches, along with elaborate theological justifications. How is this possible, and how did this situation develop historically? The essay on the image of God the Father is an attempt to answer these and other questions.

Iconographers and iconologists – I am in the latter category since God gave my mother's artistic talent to my sister – constantly speak about the canons of iconography. Although the canons they refer to are often unwritten traditions, there are many canons and ordinances which the Church has issued over the centuries. Since I ran across references to these texts nearly everywhere, I started, some time ago, to collect them for my own use. The problem was, of course, that they are all over the place, in many hard-to-find books, articles and studies. As my collection grew, I thought that others could benefit from having everything gathered in one publication. The result is the article on the canons.

Through my studies of what has been, and is being, produced by artists, I was moved to write the remaining three articles about allegory in icons, diverted looks and non-Orthodox painters. Some may think it somewhat presumptuous of me, not being a painter, to criticize the works of others. Right from the beginning of my work in this field, however, I learned that it is not sufficient to study iconography only from the point of view of art history. Since Orthodox icons constitute a theological and ecclesial art, we must examine the works with a critical, theological eye to see if they faithful express the Church's vision of faith. It is simply not enough to say that a particular image is acceptable because it was once produced somewhere or because many such images have been painted over the centuries. It has been said that an often-stated, but erroneous, theological opinion is nothing more than an old persistent heresy. The same is true for icons. Art works that claim to be icons, like written theological statements, must be submitted to critical theological scrutiny: they must be compared to the canon of Orthodox belief.

I offer these studies to those who are interested in iconography and who want to deepen their understanding of this sublime art. Since no human work is above criticism, including this one, I invite correction where necessary, a critical examination of the points of view expressed, and yet more studies to be written. I hope thereby to contribute to a greater understanding of Orthodoxy's "theology in color."

—*Fr. Steven Bigham*
*Montréal, 1994*

# THE IMAGE OF GOD THE FATHER
## IN ORTHODOX THEOLOGY AND ICONOGRAPHY

## I: INTRODUCTION

In the Orthodox Church, iconography is not primarily a question of good taste, decoration, or pedagogy. These are important, but fundamentally iconography is a reflection, in artistic forms, of the Church's dogmatic beliefs and vision. Other aspects of art are to be subordinated to the requirement of proper doctrinal reflection. As it is appropriate to judge doctrinal declarations by the canon of orthodoxy, meaning true faith and vision, it is equally appropriate to submit Church art to the same canon. It is, therefore, quite possible for there to be heterodox, even heretical, works of Church art. If the vision of the Church is not reflected in what is said or painted, the Church is obligated to make a judgment to that effect, warn the faithful of the danger, and, if necessary, formally anathematize those opinions or works of art.

Herein is the problem and theme of this study: the problem is the presence, rather widely spread, of direct representations of God the Father in Orthodox churches. These images are found either in various direct depictions of the Trinity or in historical scenes where God the Father appears in a circle in the upper part of the image. The thesis of this work is that these direct representations are alien to the Orthodox understanding of God and iconography. A corollary problem, assuming the thesis to be correct, is how it is that these images are so widely spread and have provoked so little reaction and so few calls for their removal from the churches. It is the task of this work to show that these images are alien to Holy Tradition and to provide an explanation as to why they exist, are tolerated, and even defended.

By "direct representation," we mean an image of a person, an icon, and not an indirect symbol of that person, for example a fish for Christ or keys for St. Peter. Due to the direct link between the icon and its personal prototype, we can ask the question "Who is that?" The answer can be either "That is Jesus Christ." or "That is an image of Jesus Christ." In either case, the key word in the question is "who" because it assumes that the object of the question is a person, whether human, angelic, or divine. In the case of an indirect symbol of a person, a fish, we have a direct image of some other thing, and that thing makes us think about the person, absent but hinted at in the symbol. Standing in front of a catacomb image of a fish, we cannot really ask "Who is that?" as though the question were meant to fall on the personal identity of the fish. The first question is "What is that?" and then we can ask "Who or what does that represent?" In the case of the catacomb fish, we are on fairly safe ground in assuming that the fish symbolizes Jesus Christ. No one has ever questioned the fact that there may be indirect symbolic representations of God the Father (a hand, an empty throne, etc.) but, to restate the thesis of this work, it is forbidden to make a direct representation, an icon, of the person of the Father.

One of the assumptions underlying this study is that

there is a "mind of the Church" concerning iconography. That mind does not cover all aspects of, or answer all questions about icons, but the principles are there. As there is a mind of the Church on such matters as the Trinity, the person of Christ, the divine energies, etc., a mind which has been hammered out in great historical struggles with heretical opinions and solemnly stated in ecumenical or other weighty councils, there is also a mind of the Church on iconography hammered out and solemnly set forth during the struggle with iconoclasm, 726–843. As any statement on the person of Christ must pass through Nicæa-Constantinople and accept Christ as homoousios with the Father in order to be in line with Holy Tradition, so any statement on artwork must pass through Nicæa II and its recognized interpreters in order to be considered in conformity with Holy Tradition. We hope to show that direct images, icons of God the Father, when compared to the mind of the Church on iconography are clearly unacceptable.

Another assumption underlying this presentation is the reality of the western captivity of Orthodoxy. So many authors have already treated this subject that it is not necessary to prove it here; we will take it for granted. What can be debated, however, is the extent and the legitimacy of the phenomenon. For many historical reasons, Orthodox Church life has come under the heavy influence of Roman Catholic and Protestant thought patterns, vocabulary, practices, etc., and this for several centuries and in all its local traditions: Greek, Slavic, Arabic, Rumanian, etc. The presence and justification of personal images of God the Father are, in our evaluation, directly related to this western captivity. In fact, these images are the ultimate sign of the ecclesiastical colonialism under which Orthodoxy has been living for some time. They are a serious matter because they touch on the Orthodox doctrine of God and the ways we know and do not know Him. If we say that icons are supposed to visibly reflect the theological vision we have and the life of God and His ways with man, then the presence of direct images of the Father in Orthodox churches glaringly manifests the presence of an alien vision.

Happily, in our own time we see an awakening of Orthodoxy to the state of its colonization and a re-emergence of canonical expressions of Orthodox life, theology, and iconography. We are now living through a renaissance which is permitting the reassertion of the mind of the Church in many areas of Orthodox life. Iconography is not the least of them. Precisely because of the close relation between theology and iconography, the recovery of the truly patristic mind must see itself written into canonical icons. What the recovery of the mind of the Church has allowed us to see is that in the area of iconography, there are Orthodox churches which have few if any icons in them, despite the fact that they have religious paintings covering every available wall space. Direct representations of God the Father are but the most visible symbol of a captivity from which Orthodoxy is being, and must continue to be, freed.

The mind of the Church states that the essentially invisible God became visible in the Incarnation of the Word of the Father in Jesus Christ. What was absolutely impossible before the Incarnation, that is, the making of an image of God, is now possible because the Word "became flesh and dwelt among us." Before the Incarnation, the second commandment's absolute prohibition against any images of God remained unchanged. After the Incarnation, however, that commandment was modified because the Invisible One became visible. Since visibility is part of the human nature assumed by the Word, we are therefore justified in making an image of Him. Although God manifested Himself to the saints of the Old Testament, these manifestations were different in nature from His appearing in Jesus Christ. The Old Testament theophanies were but prefigurations of the coming of Christ. They were not direct manifestations of the Father or the Holy Spirit and do not overturn the principle of the essential invisibility of God. They cannot serve as a theoretical basis of painting images of God the Father.

We will see that during the first millennium of Christian history, the Incarnation of the Word was the only theological ground on which images of God were justified. It was also in this period that the Church struggled in mortal combat with iconoclasm and solemnly set out her theology of icons. We will see also that no other direct images of God were produced except those of the person of Christ. An examination of the writings and works of art during the second millennium will show that direct images of the Trinity appeared, as well as images of God the Father alone, and that they were justified on the basis of the Old Testament theophanies. Instead of being prefigurations of the Christ, these visions were direct appearances of the Father and therefore permitted the painting of images of the Father. All the theological justifications of such images basically rest on this foundation even though they may go beyond it and incorporate arguments from psychological need or the personification of abstractions such as the divine

Wisdom. Although we know more or less when the actual images of the Father began to appear, we do not know exactly when and where the theological justifications were hammered out. What is certain, however, is that the images themselves and their theological justification are incompatible with the mind of the Church on icons. Such theological reasoning reduces the necessity and the impact of the Incarnation and thus attacks the whole structure of the Church's theological vision.

# THE IMAGE OF GOD THE FATHER
## IN ORTHODOX THEOLOGY AND ICONOGRAPHY

## 2: "SEEING GOD" IN THE BIBLE

 We cannot consider the question of images of God the Father without also considering the larger question of seeing God in general: Is God visible? How can He be seen? What do we make of the visions of God in the Bible? Since a painted image is by nature something seen, and the Father is by nature God, an image of God the Father automatically draws the two questions together. The source of all Christian thinking about God is the Bible. We therefore need to search the scriptures to see what they say about the possibility of seeing God, and what examples they give of such visions along with any interpretations of them.

If, as we claim, there comes to be a mind of the Church on iconography, and even on images of God the Father, that mind must be rooted in the scriptures. We should be able to see at least its outline if not its full elucidation. We will look at those biblical passages concerning "seeing God" to determine if any conclusions can be drawn from them, if any basic principles stand out.

## OLD TESTAMENT TEXTS ABOUT SEEING GOD

### The Angel of the Lord

There are several passages where the angel of the Lord appears to people, talks to them, and is seen by them.

The question is: Who is the angel of the Lord? In several passages, the identity of the angel seems to swing back and forth from a real angel to the Lord himself.

*Genesis 16:7-16*

> The angel of the Lord found her by a spring of water. . . . And he said, "Hagar . . . where are you going?" . . . So she called the name of the Lord who spoke to her, "Thou art a God of seeing"; for she said, "have I really seen God and remained alive after seeing him.?

*Genesis 18:*

> And the Lord appeared to him by the oak of Mamre. . . . He lifted up his eyes and looked and behold, three men stood in front of him. When he saw them, he said, "My lord. . . ." . . . and he stood by them under the tree while they ate. They said to him, "Where is Sarah . . . ?" The Lord said, " . . . your wife shall have a son. . . ." So Sarah laughed to herself. . . . The Lord said to Abraham, "Why did Sarah laugh . . . ?" . . . Then the men set out from there, and they went toward Sodom; but Abraham still stood before the Lord. Then Abraham drew near, and said, "Wilt thou indeed destroy the righteous with the wicked?" . . . And the Lord went his way when he had finished speaking. . . .

*Genesis 22:1-19:*

> . . . God tested Abraham, and said to him, "Abraham." And he said, "Here am I." . . . Then Abraham put forth his hand and took the knife to slay his son. But the angel of the Lord called to him from heaven, and said, "Abraham, Abraham. . . . you have not withheld your son, your only son, from me." . . . And the angel of the Lord called to Abraham a second time from heaven, and said, "By myself I have sworn," says the Lord . . . I will bless you."

*Judges 2:1-5:*

This text shows the identification of the angel with the Lord and the Lord himself by saying that the angel of the Lord went up from Gilgal to Bethel and said such and such; the words themselves, however, could have only been spoken by the Lord. Though the identity is made clear, there is no vision in this text.

*Judges 6 :11-24:*

> Now the angel of the Lord came and sat under the oak at
> Ophrah . . . as . . . Gideon was beating out wheat. . . And the
> angel of the Lord appeared to him and said to him, "The Lord
> is with you. . . . " . . . And the Lord turned to him and said,
> "Go . . . and deliver Israel. . . . " . . . Then the angel of the Lord
> reached out the tip of the staff that was in his hand . . . ; and the
> angel of the Lord vanished from his sight. Then Gideon per-
> ceived that he was the angel of the Lord; and Gideon said,
> "Alas, O Lord God. For now I have seen the angel of the Lord
> face to face." But the Lord said to him, " . . . do not fear, you
> shall not die."

*Judges 13:3-22:*

> And the angel of the Lord appeared to the woman and said to
> her, "Behold . . . you shall conceive and bear a son." . . . Then
> the woman came and told her husband, "A man of God came
> to me, and his countenance was like the countenance of the
> angel of God, very terrible"; . . . and the angel of God came
> again to the woman. . . . And the woman . . . told her husband,
> "Behold, the man who came to me the other day has appeared
> to me." And Manoah arose and went after his wife, and came
> to the man and said to him, "Are you the man who spoke to
> this woman.?" And he said, "I am." . . . And Manoah said to his
> wife, "We shall surely die, for we have seen God."

## The Divine Energies

In this second group of theophanies, we have manifestations of the divine energies in the form of fire,
lightening, light, etc. In general, there is no human or
angelic form seen, but only a shining. The first passage of this section forms a link with the previous one
in that the angel of the Lord appears, but only as fire.

*Exodus 3:2-6:*

> And the angel of the Lord appeared to him in a flame of fire,
> out of the midst of a bush; and Moses looked, and lo, the
> bush was burning yet it was not consumed . . . God called to

him out of the bush . . . And Moses hid his face, for he was afraid to look at God.

### Exodus 19:9-25:

The Lord said to Moses, "Lo, I am coming to you in a thick cloud that the people may hear. . . . for on the third day, the Lord will come down upon Mount Sinai in the sight of all the people. . . . " On the morning of the third day there were thunders and lightening and a thick cloud upon the mount. . . . And Mount Sinai was wrapped in smoke because the Lord descended on it in fire. And the smoke of it went up like the smoke of a kiln. . . . The Lord said to Moses, "Go down and warn the people lest they break through to the Lord to gaze and many of them perish. . . . "

### Exodus 24:16-18:

The glory of the Lord settled on Mount Sinai and the cloud of the Lord was like a devouring fire on top of the mountain in the sight of the people of Israel.

### Deuteronomy 5:23-27:

And when you heard the voice out of the midst of the darkness, while the mountain was burning with fire . . . you said, "Behold, the Lord our God has shown us his glory and greatness . . . out of the midst of the fire.

### Ezekiel 10:1-5:

Several passages in Ezekiel referring to his vision speak of the glory of the Lord as a cloud or brightness. The following passage is the most representative of them.

Then I looked, and behold, on the firmament that was over the heads of the cherubim there appeared above them something like a sapphire, in form resembling a throne. . . . And the glory of the Lord went up from the cherubim to the threshold of the house and the house was filled with the cloud and the court was full of the brightness of the glory of the Lord.

### I Kings 19:9-13:

And there he (Elijah) came to a cave and lodged there, and behold, the word of the Lord came to him. . . . And he said, "Go forth and stand upon the mount before the Lord." And behold, the Lord passed by . . . and after the fire, a still small voice. And when Elijah heard it, he wrapped his face in his mantle and went out and stood at the entrance of the cave.

## *Direct Visions*

In this group of manifestations, we have the most significant visions, those of the prophets, because they claim to have seen God directly.

*Exodus 24:9-11:*

Then Moses and Aaron, Nadab, and Abihu, and seventy of the elders of Israel went up, and they saw the God of Israel; and there was under his feet as it were a pavement of sapphire stone, like the very heaven for clearness. And he did not lay his hand on the chief men of the people of Israel; they beheld God and ate and drank.

*Numbers 12:6-8:*

And he said, "Hear my words: If there is a prophet among you, I the Lord make myself known to him in a vision, I speak with him in a dream. Not so with my servant Moses; he is entrusted with all my house. With him I speak mouth to mouth, clearly and not in dark speech; and he beholds the form of the Lord. . . .

*Isaiah 6:1-5:*

This passage is a link with the previous section because it speaks of glory and smoke and claims that Isaiah saw the Lord but does not describe any figure or form.

In the year that King Uzziah died, I saw the Lord sitting upon a throne, high and lifted up; and his train filled the temple . . . the whole earth is full of his glory . . . and the house was filled with smoke. And I saw, " . . . I am a man of unclean lips . . . my eyes have seen the King, the Lord of hosts."

*Ezekiel 1:26-28:*

And above the firmament over their heads there was the likeness of a throne, in appearance like sapphire; and seated above the likeness of a throne was a likeness as it were of a human form. And upward from what had the appearance of his loins I saw as it were gleaming bronze, like the appearance of fire enclosed round about; and downward from what had the appearance of his loins I saw as it were the appearance of fire and there was brightness round about him. Like the appearance of the bow . . . so was the appearance of the brightness round about.

### Ezekiel 8:1-5:

Then I beheld, and, lo, a form that had the appearance of a man; below what appeared to be his loins it was fire, and above his loins, it was like the appearance of brightness, like gleaming bronze.

### Daniel 7:9-15:

As I looked, thrones were placed and one that was ancient of days took his seat; his raiment was white as snow, and the hair of his head like pure wool; his throne was fiery flames, its wheels were burning fire. A stream of fire issued and came forth from before him. . . . I saw in the night visions, and behold, with the clouds of heaven there came one like a son of man and he came to the Ancient of Days and was presented before him. As for me, Daniel, my spirit within me was anxious and the visions of my head alarmed me.

## Texts Against Seeing God

### Exodus 33:18-23:

Moses said, "I pray thee, show me thy glory." And he said, "I will make all my goodness pass before you, and will proclaim before you my name 'the Lord'; . . . But," he said, "you cannot see my face; for man shall not see me and live." And the Lord said, "Behold, there is a place by me where you shall stand upon the rock; and while my glory passes by I will put you in a cleft of the rock, and I will cover you with my hand until I have passed by; then I will take away my hand, and you shall see my back; but my face shall not be seen."

### Deuteronomy 4:9-20:

Only take heed . . . lest you forget the things which your eyes have seen . . . how on the day that you stood before the Lord your God at Horeb. . . . Then the Lord spoke to you out of the midst of the fire; you heard the sound of words, but saw no form; there was only a voice. . . . Therefore take good heed to yourselves. Since you saw no form on the day that the Lord spoke to you at Horeb out of the midst of the fire. Beware lest you act corruptly by making a graven image for yourselves, in the form of any figure. . . .

### Ecclesiasticus 43:31-33:

Who has ever seen him to give a description? Who can glorify him as he deserves?

### Isaiah 40:18:

. . . to whom then will you liken God, or what likeness compare with him.?

# NEW TESTAMENT TEXTS ABOUT SEEING GOD

### John 1:18:

No one has ever seen God; the only Son, who is in the bosom of the Father, he has made him known.

### John 6:46:

Not that anyone has seen the Father except him who is from God; he has seen the Father.

### John 12:45:

And he who sees me sees him who sent me.

### John 14:8-10:

Philip said to him, "Lord, show us the Father, and we shall be satisfied." Jesus said to him, "Have I been with you so long, and yet you do not know me, Philip? He who has seen me has seen the Father; how can you say, 'Show us the Father.' Do you not believe that I am in the Father and the Father in me? . . . "

### Acts 17:29:

Being then God's offspring, we ought not to think that the Deity is like gold or silver or stone, a representation by the art and imagination of man.

### I Timothy 1:17:

To the King of ages, immortal, invisible, the only God be honor and glory for ever and ever. Amen.

*I Timothy 6:15-16:*

> . . . the blessed and only Sovereign, the King of kings and Lord of lords, who alone has immortality and dwells in unapproachable light, whom no man has ever seen or can see. To him be honor and eternal dominion. Amen.

*Colossians 1:15:*

> He is the image of the invisible God, the first born of all creation; . . .

*I John 4:11-12:*

> Beloved, if God so loved us, we also ought to love one another. No man has ever seen God; if we love one another, God abides in us and his love is perfected in us.

*Romans 1:20:*

> Ever since the creation of the world his invisible nature, namely his eternal power and deity, has been clearly perceived in the things that have been made.

## CONCLUSION ABOUT THE BIBLICAL TEXTS

The prophets did have visions and dreams of God, but their exact nature cannot be determined. In these manifestations, the prophets sometimes saw a human figure, sometimes not. Were the visions actually visual in the ordinary sense of the word? We cannot tell, but at least Daniel's description of them as "visions of my head" would suggest they were not. Other passages attempt to downplay the directness of the visions by mentioning God's being covered in smoke and clouds, Moses' being shielded from seeing God's face, Israel's hearing a voice but seeing no shape on Mount Sinai, Elijah's covering his face as God went by, etc. The basic conclusion to be drawn from the Old Testament material is that theophanies of God in human as well as other forms did take place, but at the same time the hidden, unseen, unseeable nature of God is stressed. If we stay only within the Old Testament, then the question of seeing God, and in what form, remains equivocal and inconclusive.

The New Testament witness is, however, very clear: God the Father, the divinity, is invisible, unseen, and incapable of being seen. The only one to have seen him, and make him known and seen, is Christ. In him we have the only basis of the invisible God becoming visible, of seeing God. This is, of course, the classical doctrine of the Incarnation on which the iconology of the Church is built. Little or nothing in the New Testament is said about the Old Testament visions and theophanies. We know however, that several important New Testament passages, Luke 24:44 for example, present the Old Testament as a preparation for the coming of the Word in the flesh and, therefore, we are to look for the face of Christ prefigured there.[1] It will be left to the Fathers to make clear the link between the Old and New Testaments by using the hermeneutical principle of typological prefiguration.

# THE IMAGE OF GOD THE FATHER
## IN ORTHODOX THEOLOGY AND ICONOGRAPHY

## 3: "SEEING GOD" IN THE FATHERS

We can now look at what some of the Fathers had to say about the visions of God in the Old Testament and about seeing God in general. We do not pretend to have found every possible reference to the Old Testament theophanies, but what follows is hopefully representative of the general trend of patristic thought, and, therefore, of Holy Tradition itself.

*Ignatius of Antioch:*

> Look for Christ, the Son of God who was before time, yet appeared in time, who was invisible by nature, yet visible in the flesh, who was impalpable, and could not be touched as being without a body, but for our sakes became such, might be touched and handled in the body . . .[2]

*Justin the Philosopher:*

He states quite clearly that the Father sent the Word to manifest himself to various Old Testament figures in different ways.[3] In talking about the burning bush, Justin says that the Father did not and could not have appeared; therefore, it must have been the Logos.

> He who has but the smallest intelligence will not venture to assert that the Maker and Father of all things having left all super-celestial matters, was visible on a little portion of the earth.[4]

*Theophilus of Antioch:*

Like Justin, Theophilus regarded the Old Testament theophanies as having been in fact appearances of the

Logos. God Himself cannot be contained in space and time, but it was precisely the function of the Word Whom He generated to manifest His mind and will in the created order.[5]

*Irenæus of Lyons:*

> But one and the same householder produced both Covenants, the Word of God, our Lord Jesus Christ, who spake with both Abraham and Moses. . . .[6]

> For in times long past, it was said that man was created after the image of God, but it was not actually shown; for the Word was as yet invisible, after whose image man was created . . . and He re-established the similitude after a sure manner by assimilating man to the invisible Father through means of the visible Word.[7]

> And the Word spake to Moses appearing before him . . . "then thou shalt see my back parts . . . for no man sees My face and shall live." Two facts are thus signified; that it is impossible for man to see God, and that through the wisdom of God, man shall see Him in the last times . . . that is in His coming as man.[8]

> The prophets, therefore, did not openly behold the actual face of God, but they saw the dispensations and the mysteries through which man should afterwards see God. . . . This, too, was made still clearer by Ezekiel, that the prophets saw the dispensations of God in part, but not actually God Himself. For when this man had seen the vision of God (Ezek 1:1ff) . . . and when he set forth all the rest of the visions of the thrones, lest anyone might happen to think that in those (visions) he had actually seen God, he added: "This was the appearance of the likeness of the glory of God." . . . If then neither Moses, nor Elijah, nor Ezekiel, who had all many celestial visions did see God; but if what they did see were similitudes of the splendor of the Lord and prophecies of things to come; it is manifest that the Father is indeed invisible of whom also the Lord said, "No man hath seen God at any time." But His Word, as He Himself willed it, and for the benefit of those who beheld, did show the Father's brightness and explained His purposes; . . . not in one figure nor in one character, did He appear to those seeing Him but according

to the reasons and effects aimed at in His dispensations. . . .[9]

And through the word Himself who had been made visible and palpable was the Father shown forth, although all did not equally believe in Him but all saw the Father in the Son: for the Father is the invisible of the Son, but the Son the visible of the Father.[10]

## Tertullian:

For it was the Son who descended from time to time to have converse with men, from Adam to the patriarchs and prophets, in visions, in dreams, "in a looking-glass, in an enigma," always preparing from the beginning that course which he was to follow out to the end. . . .[11]

## The Cappadocians

With Basil and the two Gregorys, we see a clear distinction made between the unknowable and invisible essence of God and the energies or operations which make Him known to us. We are not dealing anymore simply with seeing God but with knowing Him in a super-essential and mystical way. Nonetheless, the heavy emphasis on the hiddenness of the essence of God and His unapproachability fits in well with those previous Fathers who spoke of God's invisibility.

## Gregory Nazianzen:

And when I looked a little closer, I saw, not the first and unmingled Nature, known to Itself – to the Trinity. I mean . . . but only that Nature, which at last even reaches to us. And that is, as far as I can learn, the Majesty or as holy David calls it, the Glory which is manifested among the creatures, which It has produced and governs. For these are the Back Parts of God which He leaves behind Him as tokens of Himself. . . .[12]

It is difficult to conceive God but to define Him in words is an impossibility.[13]

For what will you conceive the Deity to be, if you rely upon all the approximations of reason? . . . Is He a body? How then is He the Infinite and Limitless and formless, and intangible and invisible or are these attributes of a body?[14]

And Abraham, great Patriarch, though he was justified by faith and offered a strange victim, the type of the Great Sacrifice, yet he saw not God as God but gave Him food as a man. . . . And Jacob dreamed of a lofty ladder and stair of Angels and in a mystery anointed a pillar . . . and gave to a place the name of the House of God in honor of Him whom he saw; and wrestled with God in human form; whatever this wrestling of God with man may mean. . . .[15]

What would you say of Isaiah or Ezekiel who was an eye-witness of very great mysteries and of the other prophets, for one of these saw the Lord Sabbaoth. . . . And the others described . . . Him that showed Himself in the Firmament. . . . And whether this was an appearance by day, only visible to Saints, or an unerring vision of the night or an impression on the mind holding converse with the future as if it were the present; or some other ineffable form of prophecy I cannot say; the God of the Prophets knoweth . . . but neither of these of whom I am speaking nor any of their fellows ever saw, or proclaimed the Nature of God.[16]

*John Chrysostom:*

Vladimir Lossky summarizes Chrysostom's thought from his two works *On the Incomprehensibility of God* and *On St. John* .

He (Chrysostom) also deals with the question of the vision of God in his fifteen homilies on the Gospel of St. John in which he expounded the words "no one has ever seen God." God's nature, simple, without form, without composition . . . is never an object of visions. If Isaiah, Ezekiel, and other prophets had truly seen the very essence of God, it would have appeared the same for all. God says to Hosea: "I have multiplied visions and have likened myself in the hands of the prophets " (Hos 12:10). This means, "I have not revealed my very essence, but (in visions) I condescend to the frailty of those who see me." (*Incomprehensibility*, V, 4) All that can be seen of God pertains to His condescension and not to the vision of His pure essence. . . . (*On St. John* 15:1) What is this condescension . . . ? It is the manifestation of God as He makes Himself visible "not as he is, but as he who sees him is capable of seeing by propor-

tioning the vision to the poverty of those who are seeing."
(*Incomprehensibility*, III, 3)[17]

*Eusebius of Cæsarea:*

As Von Schonborn says in summarizing Eusebius'
opinion,

> The Father uses this living instrument not only for creating
> and maintaining creatures but also for revealing himself to
> the righteous of the Old Testament. At the Oak of Mamre,
> Abraham received the visit of the Lord accompanied by two
> angels. Abraham calls "Lord" the visible figure who appears
> to him and prostrates himself before him. But who is he?
> Certainly not an angel, like the two others that accompanied
> him. Then God himself? "We must not think either that the
> God who is above all manifested himself in this way. It is not
> fitting to say that the divine changed and took on the figured
> form and look of a man. . . . We must confess therefore that
> it was the Word of God." Because God himself is ungraspable
> in a form, he uses an instrument for communicating with
> men. This is how Eusebius explains the many theophanies of
> the Old Testament.[18]

*Augustine:*

In relation to the contingent order, the three Persons
act as "one principle" (*unum principium, De trin.* 5, 15),
and "as They are inseparable, so They operate insepara-
bly" (*De trin.* 1,7 and 2,3). In his own words (*C. Maxim.*
2, 10, 2) Augustine says "where there is no difference of
natures, there is none of wills either." In illustration of
this, Augustine argues (*De trin.* 2, 12-34 and 3, 4-27)
that the theophanies recorded in the Old Testament
should not be regarded, as the earlier patristic tradition
had tended to regard them, as appearances exclusively
of the Son. Sometimes they can be attributed to the Son
or to the Spirit, sometimes to the Father, and sometimes
to all Three; on occasion it is impossible to decide to
which of the Three to ascribe them.[19] Augustine warned
against mental representations of the Father: "Avoid

conceiving of God as an old man with a very venerable look.... Do you want to see God? Stop at this thought: God is Love. What image does Love have? No one can say." (In *Epist. Joannis ad Parthos* VII, 10, PL 35, 2034a).[20]

### Theodoret of Cyrrhus:

God being incorporeal, simple and without form and not being subject to any description but having an indescribable nature, several times forms visions for the benefit of those who can see. It is possible to be manifested in one form to Abraham and in another to Moses and the same holds true for Isaiah and Ezekiel... Therefore, when you come to know the differences in these revelations, do not take the divine as having many forms but rather listen to him saying through Hosea: "I have multiplied myself in visions, and I have likened myself to the prophets according to their needs." "I have liked myself," he said, not made myself seen.... Ezekiel did not say that he had seen the Lord neither the glory of the Lord, but he has seen the likening of God's glory.... What could be more explicit than these words? [Theodoret quotes Daniel about the Son of Man coming on the clouds.] The prophet Daniel has declared these things in an evangelical and apostolic way rather than in a prophetic and riddle-like way.... This blessed Daniel has specifically taught us having foretold the second coming of Christ and explicitly calling him the Son of Man....[21]

### Diadochus of Photice:

If the prophets saw God in a physical vision, says Lossky quoting Diadochus, ...

...it is not that he appeared to them changed into a visible figure, but rather that they were among those who saw the Formless One as in the form of glory when his will and not his nature was displayed to their eyes. For it was the active will which appeared physically in the vision of glory, God having consented to let himself be seen entirely in the form of his will.[22]

We can see, then, from these early, pre-iconoclastic

writers that they do not compromise the invisibility of God, Father or Son, in the Old Testament theophanies but say that they were either dreams, riddle-like, enigmas, mysteries, similitudes, etc. The manifestations never show God as he really is but only as appearances of future things, prefigurations of the coming of the Word in the flesh. Again, as in the scriptural passages but more fully developed, we have the invisible God being made visible in Christ who was prefigured to the prophets by visions and signs. On this scriptural and patristic base, the Church will set forth her mind on iconography and images of God the Father.

# The Image of God the Father
## In Orthodox Theology and Iconography

## 4: The Iconoclastic Period

 In this chapter, we look at statements and documents which help to define the mind of the Church during the iconoclastic period. To the generally accepted dates of iconoclasm, 726–843, we add a preface and a post-script. Because some writers do not fall into the strict limits of iconoclasm but are still closely related to it, 680–870 is the range for this classical period. During this time, the Church struggled to set down clearly what and who could be painted in the Church and why. It is here that the mind of the Church was defined. It is from within this mind that we have to consider any dogmatic question concerning iconography, and the question of images of God the Father is certainly one.

We deal with eight sources in this chapter: two from the preface period, 680–726: 1) Bishop John of Thessalonica; 2) the Council of Trullo; five from the period of iconoclasm proper, 726–843: 3) Patriarch Germanos of Constantinople; 4) Pope Gregory II; 5) John of Damascus; 6) Nicæa II; 7) Theodore the Studite; and one from the post-script period in 869–70: 8) the Council of Constantinople. John of Damascus and Theodore the Studite occupy about two-thirds of the chapter because of their status as recognized interpreters, along with Nicæa II, of the mind of the Church on iconography.

*Bishop John of Thessalonica:*

Our first piece of testimony comes from a man who was a papal legate at a council in 680. Bishop John's statement carries a double weight: first because of what it says in itself and second because it was quoted with approval by the Council of Nicæa II:

> We make images of God, that is, of our Lord and Saviour Jesus Christ by painting him as he was seen on earth and as he conversed with men. We do not paint him as God. What likeness, what image could there be of the Word of God who is without body or image? For God, that is, the nature of the holy and consubstantial Trinity is spirit, as it is written; by the mercy of God the Father, his Only-Begotten Son the Word of God was incarnated for our salvation by the action of the Holy Spirit and of Mary, the All-Pure Virgin and Mother of God. We paint his humanity and not his incorporeal divinity.[23]

If the basis of painting portrait icons of God is the Incarnation of the Word of the Father, who had no image before being incarnate, then, though Bishop John does not say it specifically, no image of God the Father is possible either. He says nothing about the Old Testament visions and symbols of God, but it would be safe to say that whatever he thought, he would not have considered them as the basis on which to build an iconology permitting images of God the Father.

*The Council in Trullo:*

We next turn to the famous eighty-second canon of the Council in Trullo, also known as the Quinisext Council, in 692.[24] Like the previous statement, this canon is quoted by the Council of Nicæa II, fourth session; its authority as an expression of the mind of the Church is thus reinforced. Although we do not have in this canon a specific condemnation of images of God the Father, we do see that the Old Testament figures and shadows are not to be preferred to direct portrait icons of Christ who has now come and fulfilled all those symbols. The Council implies that they were in fact of Christ and not of the Father since it is Christ who fulfills them. These symbols are not to be despised but welcomed for what they are: prefigurations of what/who was to come. Having the choice, we should not prefer the shadow to the light. Clearly the Old Testament figures cannot be the basis of any iconography of Christ, to say nothing of the Father, that would undercut the foundation of direct portrait icons of God, the Incarnation of the Word.

> In some pictures of the venerable icons, a lamb is painted to which the Precursor points his finger, which is received as a type of grace, indicating beforehand through the law, our true Lamb, Christ our God. Embracing therefore the ancient types and shadows as symbols of the truth, and patterns given to the Church, we prefer grace and truth, receiving it as the fulfillment of the Law. In order therefore that that which is perfect may be delineated to the eyes of all, at least in colored expression, we decree that the figure in human form of the Lamb who taketh away the sin of the world, Christ our God, be henceforth exhibited in images, instead of the ancient lamb, so that all may understand by means of it the depths of the humiliation of the Word of God, and that we may recall to our memory his conversation in the flesh. . . .[25]

*Patriarch Germanos of Constantinople:*

This great Orthodox Father had the "privilege" of being patriarch when iconoclasm began as an official policy of the empire.[26] Again the basis of painting any portrait icons of God is certainly the Incarnation and as in the case of Bishop John of Thessalonica, we can infer that any direct image of God the Father would not have been accepted.

> We make no image or likeness or figure of the invisible Divinity that the sublime orders of angels cannot themselves

look on or understand: but because the Only-Begotten Son, who is in the bosom of the Father, accepted to become man by the merciful will of the Father and the Holy Spirit. . . . (because of that) we draw his human face and the image of his human form according to the flesh and not of his incomprehensible and invisible divinity.[27]

*Pope Gregory II:*

In the records of the fourth session of Nicæa II, we read two letters supposedly written by Pope Gregory II to the Emperor Leo III and sent at the beginning of the iconoclastic controversy.[28] The letters' authenticity can be questioned, but whether the Pope actually wrote them or whether they were only attributed to him is not particularly relevant here. The Fathers of Nicæa II thought they were written by him and since the Council adopted them (the contents were certainly judged worthy of an Orthodox Pope), authority was given to the ideas in the letters, if not to their historical authorship:

> Why, then, do we make no representation of God the Father? The divine nature cannot be represented. If we had seen Him, as we have seen the Son, we could also make an image of Him.[29]

In the same first letter, two other important points are underlined: the Word spoke and revealed himself in Old Testament visions and those figural images were but imperfect prefigurations of the Incarnation:

> Moses wished to see the Lord, but He showed Himself to him only from behind. To us, on the contrary, the Lord showed Himself perfectly, since the Son of God has become man . . .[30]

*John of Damascus:*

What, for John of Damascus, is the basic principle of the iconography of God? What allows us to paint portrait icons of Him? In his answer written in three apologies, *On the Divine Images*, he reflects all Orthodox thinking: the Incarnation is the decisive event that makes it possible for God to be seen and, therefore, painted. What was before the Word's becoming flesh is qualitatively different from what came after. Before the Incarnation, God is accorded all the negative, apophatic attributes which distinguish Him from the creation. After, He is given all the positive, cataphatic attributes of any human being.

> It is obvious that when you contemplate God becoming man then you may depict Him clothed in human form. When the invisible One becomes visible to flesh, you may then draw His likeness. When He who is bodiless and without form, immeasurable in the boundlessness of His own nature existing in the form of God, empties himself and takes the form of a servant in the substance and in stature and is found in a body of flesh, then you may draw His image and show it to anyone willing to gaze upon it.[31]

> In former times, God, who is without form or body, could never be depicted. But now when God is seen in the flesh conversing with men, I make an image of the God whom I see.[32]

We see that what was impossible before God became man, due to His divine nature, is now possible because the Word took on human nature. The implication here is that insofar as God the Father or the Spirit did not become man, visible, tangible, circumscribed, etc., They cannot be depicted directly in portrait icons. So what was true for the whole Trinity before Christ is now still true for the Father and the Spirit but not for the Word:

> If we attempt to make an image of the invisible God, this would be sinful indeed. It is impossible to portray one who is without body: invisible, uncircumscribed and without form.[33]

> If anyone should dare to make an image of the immaterial, bodiless, invisible, formless, and colorless Godhead, we reject it as a falsehood.[34]

Who is referred to here by the words God and God-head Who being invisible, etc. cannot be portrayed? If they do not refer specifically to the Father, then He is at least included along with the Spirit and the divine essence as undepictable since God is visible only in the Word's Incarnation. So before and after the Incarnation, God the Father's invisibility, etc. remain, precluding any iconic portraits of Him.

John of Damascus uses the word "image" to cover several kinds of representations. This is important because we need to know exactly what he is referring to when we use him to answer the question of the properness of images of God the Father. As used in the title of this work, the word "image" means a portrait icon. This is also one of the principle meanings of the term throughout the whole iconoclastic period: can we make an image, a portrait icon, of Christ and the saints? John makes some statements that give the impression of supporting the idea of an image of God (the Father), but in those passages it is clear that the meaning of the word "image" is rather symbol, type, allegorical sign, shadow, etc. and not a direct representation of the person, a portrait icon.

> The fourth kind of relative worship is given to those images which were seen by the prophets (for they saw God in the images of their visions). These images were of future things, such as Aaron's rod . . . the jar of manna . . . or the altar.[35]

> Since the creation of the world, the invisible things of God are clearly seen by means of images . . . the sun, light, burning rays, a running fountain, an overflowing river; or the mind, speech, and spirit within us; or a rose tree, a flower, a sweet fragrance.[36]

John is on very solid ground here because he is basing his point on the apophatic/cataphatic approach to knowing God set forth by Pseudo-Dionysius and other

Fathers; quoting from *The Divine Names*, chapter 1, he then comments:

> ... *through the sacred veils of the Scriptures and ecclesiastical traditions which explain spiritual truths with terms drawn from nature clothing with shapes and forms things which are shapeless and formless, and by a variety of different symbols fashioning manifold attributes of the immaterial and supernatural simplicity.*
>
> *Commentary:* If it is good for men to clothe with shape and form according to our understanding that which is shapeless, formless, and simple, shall we then not make forms and images of things which are visible and perceptible to us, that we may remember them and so be moved to imitate them.[37]

This symbolic image is clearly contrasted throughout the apologies with image meaning a portrait icon of Christ, the emperor, or the saints.

> If the image of the king is the king, and the image of Christ is Christ, and the image of a saint is the saint, and if power is not divided or glory separated, then the honor given to an image is given to the one portrayed in the image.[38]

In commenting on a quote from Gregory of Nyssa, John makes clear that he is talking about a portrait icon as opposed to a symbolic figure.

> [St. Gregory:] *Therefore human forms are what painters transfer to the canvas using various colors adding suitable and harmonious tints to the image trying with precision to capture in the image the beauty of its archetype.*
>
> *Commentary:* You see that the beauty of divinity cannot be pictured with beautiful forms, and therefore no image can be made of it; it is the human form which is transferred to the canvas by the artist's colors.[39]

It seems clear then that John of Damascus allows for images of God (the Father) in the sense of symbols and figures drawn from the empirical, sensible world which would answer the question "Who/what does that symbol represent?". He would not permit, however, an image of God the Father in the sense of a portrait icon, apart from Christ's Incarnation, an image that would answer the question "Who is that person portrayed there?". Icons are meant to show a person in his human nature. In the case of angels, who are not human, but who are sometimes represented in human form, we reach the outer limits of this iconographic principle. Angelic persons are represented, being circumscribed beings, in the human forms which they sometimes take. It is true that representations of angels as humans is a compromise between an iconology based on the representation of persons in their human natures and one based purely on symbols. However, since angels are limited, created beings, the Church's principle is preserved, though stretched, in this special case. There is no justification though for attempting to *symbolize* the uncircumscribed person of the Father in a nature totally foreign to him.

Even when discussing the visions of the Old Testament prophets along with other "images," symbols, figures, etc., John always understands them to be foreshadowings of future things connected with the Incarnation, and never as direct seeing of God in any way whatsoever; images are always typological:

Again, an image foreshadows something that is yet to happen, something hidden in riddles and shadows. For instance, the ark of the covenant is an image of the Holy Virgin and Theotokos, as are the rod of Aaron and the jar of manna.[40]

Adam . . . Jacob . . . Moses . . . Isaiah . . . and Daniel saw the likeness of a man and one like a son of man coming before the Ancient of Days. No one saw the divine nature, but the image and figure of what was yet to come.[41]

For I have seen God in human form and my soul has been saved. I gaze upon the image of God, as Jacob did, but in a different way. For he only saw with spiritual sight what was promised to come in the future, while the memory of Him who became visible in the flesh is burned into my soul.[42]

Quoting John Chrysostom approvingly as an ancient witness to this very point, John of Damascus says that "the Old Testament is a silhouette of things to come in a future age, while the New Testament is the portrait of those things."[43]

These Old Testament men saw the future in signs, figures, shadows, dreams, etc.; they did not see as we see now. The distinction between the two kinds of seeing is clear in John of Damascus: the one whose object is a symbol of the future thing and the other whose object is the person himself. It is the difference between seeing the type and seeing the archetype.

> The divine nature alone can never be circumscribed and is always without form, without shape, and can never be understood. If Holy Scripture clothes God with forms which appear to be physical or even visible shapes, these forms are still immaterial in an important sense, because they were not seen by everyone, nor could they be perceived with the unaided bodily eye, but they were seen through the spiritual sight of prophets or others to whom they were revealed.[44]

The scriptural basis for the difference between Old Testament seeing and New Testament seeing is Matthew 13:16-17; John quotes this passage putting his distinction on solid ground:

> Blessed are your eyes, for they see and your ears, for they hear. Truly, I say to you, many prophets and righteous men longed to see what you see and did not see it ... Abraham ... Moses ... Isaiah and all the prophets saw images of God but not the essence of God....[45]

How can we summarize John of Damascus' position on iconology as it relates to an image, a portrait icon of God the Father? We can say that any portrait icon of God must be based on Christ's Incarnation; that is the sole basis of seeing God and painting his direct, personal image. Though God has revealed himself in the Old Testament in symbols, types, and "images" of future events, these cannot be considered portraits of God. In the case of the prophets who "saw" the form of a man, their manner of seeing was qualitatively different from the apostles in seeing Christ and ours in seeing an icon of Christ. What they "saw" was a prefiguration of Christ's coming in the flesh and not God the Father. The conclusion seems obvious: there is no basis in John of Damascus for a portrait icon or a symbolic image in human form of God the Father:

> Therefore, I boldly draw an image of the invisible God, not as invisible but as having become visible for our sakes partaking of flesh and blood. I do not draw an image of the immortal Godhead, but I paint the image of God who became visible in the flesh, for if it is impossible to make a representation of a spirit, how much more impossible is it to depict the God who gives life to the spirit.[46]

*The Council of Nicæa II:*

In its sixth session, the Seventh Ecumenical Council took up the theme of the visibility and paintability of God based on the Incarnation. Although not specifically referred to in the text, portrait icons of God the Father would certainly have been excluded:

> Christians have never given worship in spirit and in truth to images nor to the divine figure of the cross. They have never made an image of the invisible and incomprehensible nature, but it is only in so far as the Word became flesh and dwelt among us that we paint the mysteries of man's redemption.[47]

*Theodore the Studite:*

We consider Theodore's iconology as contained in his three writings, *On the Holy Icons*. One term which is at the heart of his iconology is the word *circumscribed*. John of Damascus does use the term but not nearly as much as does Theodore. It is on practically every page and whole sections are dedicated to its meaning. We can see from his presentation that the distinction *circumscribed/uncircumscribed* is the basis on which portrait icons of God are possible: that which is circumscribed is paintable and that which is uncircumscribed is not. What, though, does he mean by this term and its negation? Proceeding according to the *apophatic/cataphatic* method, Theodore defines as circumscribed everything that is in creation. The term has the sense of being limited in some way by the various dimensions of the created order. These dimensions are then negatively attributed to God: "There are many kinds of circumscription – inclusion, quantity, quality, position, places, times, shapes, bodies – all of which are denied in the case of God, for divinity has none of these."[48] One undisputable dimension of the creation is visibility. If something is visible in the normal physical sense, then it must be circumscribed. Though things can be circumscribed and invisible, angels for example, nothing uncircumscribed can be seen.

It is a rather simple step from this idea of circumscription to designating God as uncircumscribed and men as circumscribed: God is uncreated and limitless, and man is created and limited. The basic principle of iconography, then, is that anything circumscribed can be painted, and anything uncircumscribed cannot. Since only God is uncircumscribed, He cannot be painted in any way. But when the Word becomes flesh, then He takes on circumscription and is visible and paintable:

> There is a mixture of the immiscible, a compound of the uncombinable: that is of the uncircumscribable with the circumscribed, of the boundless with the bounded, of the

limitless with the limited, of the formless with the well formed (which is indeed paradoxical). For this reason Christ is depicted in images, and the invisible is seen. He who in His own divinity is uncircumscribable accepts the circumscription natural to His body.[49]

For creation is a property of circumscription. . . . If every image is an image of form, shape, or appearance and of color and if Christ has all these, since the Scriptures say, "He took the form of a servant . . . and was found in human shape," and had an "ignoble and inferior" appearance, which signifies the body; then He is portrayed in just such a circumscription in His likeness.[50]

Though Christ's circumscription may seem to be obvious to us, so many centuries after the controversy, it was not so obvious at the time of the iconoclastic controversy. Theodore the Studite and others had to argue that in fact the Incarnation meant that Christ is truly limited, visible, tangible, etc. in his humanity. The iconoclasts did believe that Christ had become truly man, but somehow the fact that He came from the Father overshadowed His human circumscription, or at least compromised it, and so excluded portraying Him in limited art forms:

An objection as from the Iconoclasts: "If the Son is the perfect image of the Father, so that the Father appears in Him, as the Scripture says, 'He who has seen me has seen the Father,' we must say that He who comes from the uncircumscribable Father is uncircumscribable. For how could that which is uncircumscribable even be seen in that which is circumscribed?"

Answer: If He who comes from the uncircumscribable Father is uncircumscribable, then obviously He who comes from a circumscribed mother is circumscribed. . . . But if both are true of the one Christ, then He has also acquired the properties of both origins and is uncircumscribable and circumscribed.[51]

As well as establishing Christ's circumscription in His

humanity, this passage clearly states that the Father is, and remains after as well as before the Incarnation, uncircumscribed. This is important because it makes clear that God the Father is invisible, unbounded, etc. and therefore unpaintable. No portrait icon of Him is possible because He has never been seen or can be seen, His uncircumscribed divine nature preventing any direct representation.

In discussing artificial and natural images, Theodore makes it very clear that the Father can have no artificial image or portrait icon:

> In respect to His coming forth from the uncircumscribable Father, since He is uncircumscribable, he would not have an artificial image: with what likeness can the Godhead be composed, for which the divine Scripture utterly forbids any representation?[52]

This passage and others raise a question, also present in John of Damascus, of the relationship of God the Father and the Godhead. An objection might be made that what these two writers forbid is an image of divinity, the divine nature as distinguished from the Father as a divine person. The problem is one of vocabulary and of theology. First of all, we know that though the two terms, nature and person, are distinguishable, they are not separable. We cannot speak of divinity by itself except as enhypostasized in the person of the Father. No separation is possible that might allow a representation of the Father's person apart from his nature or vice versa.

Secondly, in dealing with the vocabulary of both writers, we have several terms to deal with: God, the Word, Christ, the Son, Man, humanity, etc. Theodore uses them in different contexts depending on the statement of the iconoclasts or his own point, but in all these cases, there is one line of demarcation which remains clear throughout his writings: the line between what is uncircumscribable and what is circumscribable. Applying this distinction to the vocabulary, the terms fall into place. God, Godhead, God the Father, divinity, divine nature, Word (before the Incarnation) are all on the uncircumscribable side; Man, humanity, Christ and Word (after the Incarnation) are on the circumscribable side. On the one side, artificial images, portrait icons, are impossible while on the other, they are possible. The uncircumscribable side can, however, be represented by "images" in John of Damascus' sense, i.e., by allegorical symbols. An angel (the Hospitality of Abraham), fire, light, the empty space between the cherubim on the ark, an empty throne, etc. can represent God the Father, but these symbols are not portrait icons directly representing His person in His nature but only pointers to God's invisible presence. They are in fact images of other things but turn our thoughts to the Father. The Word made flesh is the link between the two sides allowing the uncircumscribable to have an artificial image – a portrait icon of Jesus Christ.

Let us turn now to the question of the appearances and "images" of God in the Old Testament. We will see that Theodore the Studite follows John of Damascus' opinion in considering the visions and revelations of God in the Old Testament as manifestations and prefigurations of the Word, not of the Father:

An apparent contradiction suggests that Christ is not circumscribed, because the Scripture says, "You heard the sound of words, but saw no form; there was only a voice." If Moses says, speaking about the God of all, "you heard the sound of words, but saw no form; there was only a voice," and Isaiah on the other hand says, "We saw Him, and He had no form or beauty; but His appearance was ignoble, and inferior to all the children of men," how will these prophets agree with each other, if indeed one does not conflict with the other? Clearly both are speaking of the same one. Moses is denying that the Godhead can be in a likeness, for divinity is invisible and therefore unlike anything, Isaiah is affirming in reference to the same Lord who took the form of a servant, that He is seen in appearance like ours.[53]

We can also say that Theodore stands squarely with previous writers in that he sees all the signs, symbols, figures, etc. set out in the Old Testament as types and prefigurations in a veiled fashion of Christ and the economy of grace:

> First I will say this, that whatever the Law says it says to those under the Law. The ancient commandments should not be imposed on those under grace. If they were, we would keep the Sabbath and be circumcised; many things contrary to our faith would follow. But we must understand these things only as a foreshadowing. The apostle says that the Law is a shadow but not the true image of the realities.[54]

In speaking of the bronze serpent and the cherubim on the ark, Theodore says:

> Now you see the whole teaching of Scripture; although the angels are not solid like us; and although the serpent differs from us by its reptilian shape, nevertheless it was received figuratively as a symbol of Christ. If God formerly condescended to be symbolized by a serpent in order to heal those who were bitten, how could it not be pleasing to Him and appropriate to set up the image of the bodily form which has been His since He became man?[55]

A clearer distinction could not be asked for between images as symbols and types, and images as portrait icons, precisely the distinction made by John of Damascus.

And finally, we see that Theodore the Studite quotes the eighty-second canon of Trullo where the New Testament image, the portrait icon, of Christ is to be substituted for the Old Testament figure of the lamb. Since the shadow of the Law has passed away with the coming of grace and truth, Christ; those Old Testament types and symbols of Him are no longer necessary. The two orders of images are clearly accepted and though they are welcomed and venerable, they must be replaced by the artificial image, the portrait icon, of the One who is Himself the fulfillment of those prefigurations.

In summary, we can see that Theodore is in agreement with John of Damascus in defining the mind of the Church on iconography. The Incarnation, the circumscribing of the Word, is the basis of our seeing and painting God's portrait, and the prophetic visions as well as all the signs and figures are manifestations of the Word and not of the Father: in no way, then, can they be set up as shadowy rivals to Christ's true image, the portrait icon.

*The Council of Constantinople 843:*

In 843, the final defeat of iconoclasm took place and a local council of Constantinople restored all the icons and inaugurated the liturgical feast of the Triumph of Orthodoxy. This council and the new feast were the crowning confirmation of the Church's mind against iconoclasm.

In the Synodicon of Orthodoxy set out by this council, we have a succinct statement of the basis of seeing and painting God:

> to those who have received from God the force to distinguish between the prohibition contained in the Law and the teaching brought by Grace: that is, on the one hand, what in the Law is invisible, and on the other, what according to Grace, is visible and palpable, [to those] who for that very reason represent visible and touchable realities in images and venerate them, memory eternal.[56]

In one of the anathemas of the Synodicon, we have a rather complicated statement about the Old Testament prophets and their visions. It is put negatively, but the sense is clear: if you accept the prophetic visions as figures and images of Christ before the Incarnation and do not accept the images of the Word made flesh after the Incarnation, then you deserve to be excluded from the Church:

> Those who admit . . . the visions of the prophets but reject the paintings they saw . . . before the Incarnation of the Word or who agree that these spectacles were shown to the visionaries as an image, figures, and sketches of the truth, but refuse to represent the incarnate Word or his suffering for us in an image, let them be anathema.[57]

### The Council of Constantinople 869–70:

As there was a preface to the iconoclastic period in the form of the statements of John of Thessalonica and the Council in Trullo, there was also a kind of postscript in the form of the Council of Constantinople, 869–70. Although not considered as ecumenical by the Orthodox Church – it is considered the eighth council by the Roman Catholic Church – it reaffirmed the decisions of Nicæa II and helped stamp out any remaining coals of iconoclasm. Specifically, its third canon requires the image of Christ to have veneration equal with that of the gospel book. The question of an image of God the Father is not dealt with directly, but as in many previous statements, the kinds of permitted icons are enumerated. The image of God the Father, however, is not among them:

> If anyone does not venerate the image of Christ our Lord, let him be deprived of seeing him in glory at his second coming. The image of his all pure Mother and the images of the holy angels as well as the images of all the saints are equally the object of our homage and veneration.[58]

There are two final pieces of evidence, of a quasi-documentary nature. Both are arguments from silence and in themselves should not carry determining weight. However, after the positive evidence already presented, they have their place. The first point is that throughout the entire iconoclastic period, there is never once a mention of actually existing images of God the Father or of direct representations of the Trinity. Those who can be represented in icons are exclusively Christ, Mary, the prophets, the saints, and the angels. The second point is that the iconoclasts never charge the Orthodox with idolatry because they venerate an image of the Trinity or of God the Father. Knowing the iconoclastic reaction to the veneration of Christ in an icon, we can imagine that they would not have let pass a chance to attack the Orthodox on the basis of images of God the Father or of direct representations of the Trinity. No such charge is ever heard from them on this subject. Such deafening silence in the light of the statements in this chapter should not be surprising. It is just another witness to the fact that in the mind of the Church, there is no place for direct images of God the Father.

# THE IMAGE OF GOD THE FATHER
## IN ORTHODOX THEOLOGY AND ICONOGRAPHY

## 5:THE LITURGICAL WITNESS

The living experience of the Christian sacramental and liturgical life is a primary source of Christian doctrine. . . . In
addition to the living experience of the Liturgy, the texts of
the services and sacraments provide a written source of doctrine in that they may be studied and contemplated by one
who desires an understanding of Christian teaching.[59]

The mind of the Church is expressed as much
in her liturgical texts and hymns as in the
writings of the Fathers and the decisions of
councils. In this chapter, we examine some liturgical texts that shed light on the question of images of
God the Father. It is not possible to consider every perti-
nent liturgical text used by the Orthodox Church, but
those considered here show what has already been established as the mind of the Church: the basis of any
portrait icons of God is the Incarnation of the Word, excluding by implication images of the non-incarnate
Father. By further implication, the Old Testament "images" and figures of God cannot be set up as rivals to the
Incarnation as the basis of our seeing God and painting
His portrait icon. We see, again, that the liturgical texts
claim that the Old Testament is full of many
prefigurations of the Incarnation and that the prophets
did not "see" God the Father but the Word. In this chapter, we use the *Lenten Triodion*, the *Pentecostarion*, and
the *Festal Menaion*. The bulk of the liturgical texts contained in these three collections gives a representative

sampling of what we would find if all the liturgical material were combed for relevant statements.

The first thing to note is that there are few if any direct statements about images of God the Father. As in the classical period of the formation of the mind of the Church, the lack of direct statements is an argument from silence that in fact such images were never contemplated and so references to them or a theology to support them never entered into the liturgical texts. The texts do make clear, however, that we can now see openly and directly what was invisible before the Incarnation and "visible" only in signs and figures. Direct seeing is now possible as a result of the Incarnation of the Word.

## THE INVISIBLE MADE VISIBLE
### BY THE INCARNATION

*Nativity according to the Flesh, Lity:*
> Heaven and earth are united today, for Christ is born. Today has God come upon earth and man gone up to heaven. Today for man's sake is seen in the flesh He who by nature is invisible. . . .[60]

*Orthodoxy Sunday, Saturday evening at Little Vespers, stichera:*
> He who is invisible by nature and without beginning showed himself as a mortal man, O Virgin, coming from your most chaste womb because of his extreme goodness, and having thus drawn his bodily representation, we the faithful bow down before him. . . .[61]

*Sunday of the Publican and the Pharisee, Matins, ninth ode:*
> It is impossible for men to see God on whom even the angels do not dare look, but to mortal men the Word made flesh showed himself thanks to you, O Most Pure One. . . .[62]

*Holy Monday, Matins, second cathisma:*
> O invisible Judge, thy Incarnation made you visible to our

eyes, . . . Honor and glory to your power, O Word of God.[63]

*Kontakion for Orthodoxy Sunday:*

> No one could describe the Word of the Father; but when he took flesh from you, O Theotokos, he consented to be described and restored the fallen image to its former state by uniting it to divine beauty. We confess and proclaim our salvation in word and images.[64]

Though there is nothing about an image of God the Father and relatively little about the Incarnation as the basis of seeing the invisible, there is a wealth of texts which set forth three other important points: 1) the Word, and not the Father, revealed Himself to the Old Testament prophets; 2) the Incarnation of the Word is prefigured in the prophets' dreams, visions, signs, figures, etc.; and 3) these dark, dreamy, and unclear manifestations were illuminated and superseded by Christ's coming in the flesh. Though the texts do not reject the Old Testament signs and figures as a basis of iconography, of seeing God, they strongly imply the inferiority of those figures when set beside the Word seen in the flesh and painted in portrait icons. We hear clear echoes of canon eighty-two of the Council in Trullo in these texts; they contrast the dim Old Testament prefigurations with the clear, bright revelation of God the Word incarnate. These texts, therefore, can only be taken as a buttress to the Church's mind on iconography.

## CHRIST THE WORD MADE KNOWN IN THE OLD TESTAMENT

*Forefeast of the Nativity of Christ, Compline, seventh canticle:*

> The profane command of a lawless tyrant fanned the flames exceedingly high; but Christ cast the dew of the Spirit over

the children who feared God. . . .[65]

*Forefeast of Theophany, Compline, eighth canticle:*

Be ye astonished, O ye heavens. . . . For lo He who once made the sacrifice of His righteous prophet burn most wondrously with water [1 Kings 18:35-6] wraps Himself in the water of Jordan.[66]

*Sunday of the Myrrhbearers, Midnight Office, fifth ode:*

Thou didst appear to Moses in the burning bush in the form of fire, O Word of the Father, and under the name of Angel of God to show thy presence clearly among us and announce the triple reign of thy unique divinity.[67]

*Transfiguration, Great Vespers, apostica:*

He who once spoke through symbols to Moses on Mount Sinai saying "I am He who is" was transfigured today on Mount Tabor before the disciples. . . .[68]

*The Meeting of the Lord, Great Vespers, stichera:*

Receive, O Simeon, Him whom Moses once beheld in darkness granting the Law on Sinai . . . and this is He who spoke through the Law . . . this is He whose voice was heard in the prophets, who for our sakes has taken flesh and has saved man. . . .[69]

# CHRIST "SEEN" IN
# OLD TESTAMENT VISIONS

*Birth of the Theotokos, Matins, fifth canticle:*

O ye people, let us sing the praises of the Cause of all things, who caused Himself to become like unto us. Counted worthy to behold the images that prefigured Him, the prophets rejoiced and now they enjoy as fruit His manifest salvation.[70]

*Forefeast of the Nativity of Christ, Compline, ninth canticle*

As far as it was right, Thou wast seen by the prophets. Made man in the last times, Thou hast appeared to all in Bethlehem. . . .[71]

*The Meeting of the Lord, Lity:*

The Ancient of Days, who in times past gave Moses the Law

on Sinai appears this day as a babe. . . . Today Simeon takes in his arms the Lord of Glory whom Moses saw in the darkness. . . . This is He who speaks through the prophets. . . .[72]

*The Meeting of the Lord, Lity:*

The Ancient of Days a young child in the flesh, was brought to the temple by His mother. . . .[73]

*The Meeting of the Lord, Matins, sessional hymn:*

The Ancient of Days for my sake becomes a child. . . .[74]

*The Meeting of the Lord, Matins, third canticle, sessional hymn:*

Moses in days of old saw on Mount Sinai the back parts of God and was counted worthy in darkness and a storm of wind faintly to hear the divine voice. But now Simeon has taken in his arms God who for our sakes took flesh. . . .[75]

*The Meeting of the Lord, Matins, fifth canticle:*

In a figure Isaiah saw God upon a throne lifted up on high borne in triumph by angels . . . and he cried, "Woe is me for I have seen beforehand God made flesh. . . ."[76]

*Fifth Sunday of Lent, Matins, ninth ode:*

Going beyond nature and its laws, you gave birth in a marvelous way, as a newborn child, to the Law Giver of the world and the Ancient of Days. Being the mystical Heaven of the Creator of the universe, with love we the faithful magnify you.[77]

# THE INCARNATION FULFILLS OLD TESTAMENT SIGNS AND FIGURES

*Birth of the Theotokos, Matins fifth canticle:*

Thou hast scattered the dim shades of dark sayings and hast illuminated the hearts of the faithful by the coming of the truth through the Child of God: Guide us also by thy light, O Christ.[78]

*Entry of the Theotokos, Matins, fourth canticle, second canon:*

O prophet Habakkuk, thou hast foreseen in spirit the Incarnation of the Word and hast proclaimed crying: Thou shalt be acknowledged when the years draw nigh. . . .[79]

*Forefeast of the Nativity of Christ, Compline, third canticle:*

O merciful Lord, making manifest the figures of Thine ineffable Incarnation, Thou hast unfolded visions and breathed forth prophecies; and now Thou art come and hast fulfilled them being born in the flesh from a pure Maid. . . .[80]

*Nativity according to the Flesh, Matins, ninth canticle, second canon:*

We have seen, O pure Mother, the dim figures of the Word and the shades that are past. And now that He has newly appeared from the closed gate, we who are counted worthy to behold the Light of truth . . . bless thy womb.[81]

*Forefeast of Theophany, Compline, third canticle:*

Figures of Thy theophany hast Thou shown in times past to the prophets; but now hast Thou revealed in visible activity and operation the mysteries that were hidden, making Thyself manifest to men today and dispensing a new regeneration.[82]

*Forefeast of Theophany, Matins, sixth ode:*

For this cause shalt thou have such honor as belong not to the angels, and I shall make thee greater than the prophets. Not one of them saw Me openly, but only in figures and shades and dreams, while thou hast seen Me standing of Mine own will before thee. . . .[83]

*Orthodoxy Sunday Vespers, stichera:*

The grace of truth has shown forth: what was before darkly prefigured, now is brought about in bright daylight. . . .[84]

*First Week of Lent, Friday Evening, Service of Kolyva:*

By symbols and figures, by various images and enigmas, the prophets revealed beforehand, O Virgin, your birthgiving, a marvel that goes beyond nature: we therefore sing to you . . . exalting Christ throughout all the ages.[85]

We also note that in the various books containing blessings (*Trebnik, The Book of Needs, Evchologion,* and *Evchologe*), the categories of icons reflect those set out in the classical statements: icons of the saints, of the Mother of God, of Christ and His feasts, and of the Trinity. For Trinity icons, the title of the section reads, in translation: "The Blessing of an Icon of the Holy Trinity, Represented by the Three Angels, the Feasts of the Theophany, the Transfiguration, and the Descent of the Holy Spirit."[86] These prayers reflect very well the mind of the Church: the only proper images of the Trinity are indirect representations of historical events in which we sense but do not see the trinitarian presence. This liturgical witness is even more important because of the ancient principle of *lex orandi lex credendi*: the law of prayer is the law of belief. The Church continues to pray her mind on this question even though the actual production of icons often betrays it.

It is clear, then, from the liturgical texts cited above that those who wish to defend portrait icons of God the Father will find no support from this source: the Incarnation is the basis of seeing God and of painting his icons, and it is Christ, not the Father, who is prefigured in the Old Testament. Any other iconographic foundation is a dangerous innovation with no foundation in Holy Tradition.

## 6: Three Russian Councils

About seven centuries after the classical period during which the Church's mind concerning iconography had been formed and expressed, a series of Russian church councils occurred which deal very specifically with images of God the Father. These councils, and their decisions, are of great importance because they took place at the beginning of the period when the Orthodox Church was coming under heavy Catholic and Protestant influence. They are important not only because of their dates but even more for what they said. Even as the western influence was penetrating the Orthodox mentality, we see that the Church in Russia was able to respond to specific questions of iconography from within her own mind.

It may be said that these councils were only local and Russian, and therefore, they do not merit great attention, not being ecumenical. It is true, of course, that they were not ecumenical, but their importance should not thereby be slighted. These councils applied the Church's mind to new questions, and rendered decisions in general conformity with that mind. We say "general conformity" because certain elements in these councils sound a discordant note. The question here is not whether these councils were local or ecumenical but whether or not they expressed the mind of the Church on a question of iconography. If they did, they should be acclaimed; if not, they should be forgotten. These, then, are the three councils: 1) The Stoglav Council of Moscow, 1551; 2) the Council of Moscow, 1553–54; and 3) the Great Council of Moscow, 1666–67.

## THE STOGLAV COUNCIL OF MOSCOW, 1551

In order to respond to specific and general religious questions and also to examine the whole of Russian Church life, Tsar Ivan III called a council in Moscow in 1551. It has received the name of Stoglav because its decisions were written up in one-hundred chapters, the meaning of the Russian word *stoglav*. Among other things, we see a constant theme running throughout the one-hundred chapters of this council: icons are to be painted according to accepted, consecrated models, with no fantasy or novelty allowed:

> You must watch and be sure that iconographers instruct their students and teach them to paint images with artfulness and according to the consecrated model. . . .[87]

> The ancient traditions of the holy Fathers, the famous iconographers, both Greek and Russian, bear witness. . . .[88]

> On the holy churches, a cross is to be placed according to the holy rules. . . . Let the crosses that have been erected and set in place remain there as in the past. . . .[89]

> The painter . . . [should] paint with scrupulous care . . . according to the consecrated model.. . . .[90]

> Those who up to the present have been painting icons with no artfulness, according to their own fantasies and manner, without any concern for the likeness, the paintings of those who paint in this manner should be taken away. . . .[91]

> Each prelate in his diocese is to be vigilant and to pay untiring attention to make sure that good iconographers and their students reproduce the ancient models, that they refrain

from all fantasy, that they do not represent God in just any old way. If Christ our God has been represented in his fleshly envelope, the Divinity is hidden to all painters. St. John of Damascus said, "Do not represent the Divinity; do not give him a false form, you blind men, because the Divinity cannot be captured by your eyes. It is impenetrable to your gaze. . . ."[92]

In this passage from chapter forty-two of the Stoglav Council, we have the partial answer given to two of the questions asked by Tsar Ivan III: 1) How should the halo be painted on the icons of the Hospitality of Abraham used as a symbolic image of the Trinity? 2) What should be the title painted on the icon? According to the Tsar, the ancient icons had no cross inscribed on the halo of the central angel representing Christ, and the only title written was "The Holy Trinity" and not "The Holy Trinity" plus "Jesus Christ" near the central angel.

> The fathers of the council agreed completely with the Tsar and gave the following answer: "The iconographers are to reproduce the ancient models, those of the Greek iconographers, of Andrei Rublev, and of the famous painters. 'The Trinity' is to be written on top of the icon." They added that "painters must not follow their fantasy in anything."[93]

We have here the meaning of "the consecrated model" in reference to the images of the Trinity: Rublev's icon of the Hospitality of Abraham based on classical Byzantine models is to be the proper Orthodox representation of the Trinity. Since this scene is of an historical event in the Old Testament, the visit of the three mysterious persons to Abraham and Sarah at the Oak of Mamre, we do not have a direct representation of any of the persons of the Trinity. We do not have any portrait icons but rather images which fall into the category of the types, figures, and prefigurations of the Old Testament. In attempting to

deal with the Trinity iconographically, we are limited
to this symbolic level because the Trinity has not
been manifested in such a way as to permit a direct
representation, a portrait icon. The New Testament
images of the Transfiguration, Theophany, and Pentecost are in the same category; they are images of
historical events with a specific trinitarian content.

Since we have, in the icon of the Hospitality of
Abraham, an historical event, those elements which
show its historical character ought not to be ne-
glected. Thus Abraham, Sarah, the oak, etc. should
appear in the icon. Any attempt to de-emphasize the
historical, giving the impression of a direct representation should not be encouraged. By maintaining the
distinction between an historical event serving as a
symbol and a direct portrait icon, we can receive the
decision of the Stoglav Council as being in full conformity with the mind of the Church. Ostrogorsky is
of the same opinion:

> ... we see that the Council of One Hundred Chapters tried
> to maintain this way of representing the Trinity and thus to
> block any attempt at painting God the Father on Trinity
> icons, as was being done in the West.[94]

## THE COUNCIL OF MOSCOW, 1553–54

The second council to be considered was presided
over by the same Metropolitan Makary who presided
at the Stoglav Council. The 1553 council again considered the question of images of God the Father. This
time state secretary Viskovatyj protested the appearance of direct representations of God the Father in
so-called Trinity icons which had recently been introduced in some Moscow churches. He felt that such

images were alien innovations, imports to be rejected as unorthodox.

> Metropolitan Makary himself tried to dispel the doubts raised by Viskovatyj and saw nothing wrong in representing God the Father in icons illustrating the Nicene Creed, for example; he tried to explain that representing God in the form in which he appeared to the prophets in their visions, in no way means that iconographers paint the uncircumscribed Divinity. . . . He said finally that these icons are not innovations but are painted according to models.[95]

The reasoning of Metropolitan Makary was accepted at this council, Viskovatyj was condemned, and for about one hundred years the two councils stood opposed to each other giving a confused answer to the question of images of God the Father.

A common theme of both councils, however, is their appeal to "the consecrated models." In a sense Metropolitan Makary was right; the image of God the Father in so-called Trinity icons had been established for a long time, not in the iconography of the Orthodox Church, but rather in western, Latin religious art. He at least felt obliged to justify such images on the basis of "the consecrated model." Assuming that he could have been shown that this kind of image was an innovation imported from the West, the Metropolitan would probably have disallowed it. But his acceptance of these images does not rest only on the argument from tradition. If that were all, he could be excused for simply not knowing his art history.

A more serious problem is the Metropolitan's flawed reasoning. Let us look at the pillars of his argument. For the Metropolitan, painting God the Father directly is simply an illustration of an article of the Nicene Creed: "I believe in one God the Father Almighty." As an artist might illustrate a passage from the gospels to make it more vivid in the mind of the hearers, an iconographer can illustrate the creed by putting into visual form the meaning of Father. We see here that an Orthodox prelate was able to view a question about iconography simply from the point of view of illustration. He apparently saw no dogmatic matter involved in the question at all. Though biblical illustrations are by no means insignificant, the Orthodox Church's mind considers narrative illustration as a secondary motive for Church art.

Another pillar of the Metropolitan's argument is based on the Old Testament visions given to the prophets. He felt that God the Father could be directly portrayed because He had appeared, had been seen in these visions. We have already seen, however, that the mind of the Church does not consider these visions as "seeing" in the same sense as seeing in the New Testament. And further, they are not revelations of the Father but prefigurations of the Incarnation of the Word.

The final pillar of the Metropolitan's argument comes from a separation between the divinity and the person of the Father. This separation allows the symbolic illustration of the word Father without at the same time representing his divinity. Orthodoxy knows well the distinction between person and nature so that we can say that the Word and the Spirit have the same nature as the Father but are different persons. Such a distinction, however, as would allow the person of the Father to be represented but not in the only nature He has, His divinity, is a point of view alien to the Orthodox vision. These arguments will be seen again as the main Roman Catholic defense of direct images of the Trinity. Whether Metropolitan Makary's opinions are direct importations from the West, which seems most likely, or whether he independently thought them up himself, their contrast with the mind of the Church is too striking to be missed.

As we might think, looking at the arguments he gave to the council in 1553, Metropolitan Makary represented a certain mind set that, for the question at hand, was already moving Russia away from the ancient iconographic traditions of Byzantium.[96]

## THE GREAT COUNCIL
## OF MOSCOW, 1666–67

The third council is the great reform council of 1666–67, at which again the question of images of God the Father came up. This council minced no words and made a ringing declaration of the mind of the Church, with one slight hitch, however. We cite the whole canon "On Iconographers and God Sabbaoth" due to the importance of its content:

> To write an icon of the Lord Sabbaoth, which is the same thing as the Father with a gray beard along with his only begotten Son in his bosom and a dove between them, is very bad and inappropriate for no one has seen the Father in his divinity: for the Father does not have flesh and the Son was not incarnately born from the Father before the ages. As the Prophet David says, "from before the morning watch, I have begotten thee." So this birth is not according to the flesh, but unspeakable and incomprehensible. And also Christ himself says in the holy gospel: "No one knows the Father but the Son. . . .", and Isaiah the prophet says, "to whom could you liken God? What image could you contrive of him?" The same thing is also said by the holy apostle Paul in Acts 17:29: "since we are the children of God, we have no excuse for thinking that the Deity looks like anything in gold, silver, or stone that has been carved and designed by man." And as St. John of Damascus said, "No one can make an imitation of the invisible and incorporeal and indescribable and unimaginable God; only a pure lunatic and totally unpious person would do such a thing." In the same way, St. Gregory the Dialogos, Pope of Rome, forbids the same thing. Because of these preceding statements, we are supposed to understand the divinity of Sabbaoth and the eternal birth of the only be-

gotten Son from the Father in our mind, but it is not possible and is inappropriate to write images of them. The Holy Spirit is not a dove according to essence but God by essence, and no one has ever seen God, as St. John the Evangelist and Theologian witnesses. Only at the Jordan at the holy baptism of Christ did the Holy Spirit appear in the form of a dove, and for this reason it is permissible to write an image of the Holy Spirit in the form of a dove for this icon. In any other place, it is not permitted to write the Holy Spirit in the form of a dove. Also he appeared on Mt. Tabor as a cloud and sometimes in other forms. In addition, the name Sabbaoth is applied not to the Father but only to the Holy Trinity. According to Dionysius, Sabbaoth is translated from Hebrew, the language of the Jews, as the "the Lord of Hosts," and thus "Lord of Hosts" is the Holy Trinity: Father, Son, and Holy Spirit. Also the Prophet Daniel says, "I have seen the Ancient of Days sitting on the judgment seat," and this is applied not to the Father but to the Son because he will be judging every nation with his fearful judgment at his Second Coming. Also some write Sabbaoth on the icons of the Holy Annunciation as he is breathing from his mouth, and this breath is going to the womb of the most Holy Theotokos. Who has ever seen such a thing or what holy scripture witnesses to that? Where is it taken from? It is very clear that this practice and similar practices come from people who possess foolish wisdom or, more properly to stated, are crazy. On the basis of the preceding, we order from henceforth that this inappropriate and foolish practice stop. Only in Revelations, because of necessity, is the Father written with gray hair. It is right and appropriate to put a crucifix on the iconostase, that is a cross which shows the Lord and Saviour Jesus Christ instead of Sabbaoth. And this order is in effect in all the holy churches in the eastern countries and in Kiev and all over the principality of Moscow. This great mystery is set forth in the holy churches. As Moses erected a bronze serpent in the desert as an image of the Saviour Christ so that any Jew bitten by snakes was healed by looking at it, in the same way we who are the new Israel while looking at the crucifix and the passion of our Saviour Jesus Christ in the holy churches are healed from the bites of the invisible serpent, the devil, these bites being our sins.[97]

This canon needs little explanation and its message is in clear and evident conformity with the mind of the Church formed during the iconoclastic period. The "slight hitch" in the thinking of the council is found in its statement about Revelations: "Only in Revelations, because of necessity, is the Father written with gray hair.". Ouspensky calls this "the incoherence of the thinking characteristic of this period."[98] After a ringing declaration of the mind of the Church, we read that the Father can in fact be represented with "gray hair . . . of necessity." The text referred to is Revelations 1:13-14: "when I turned I saw . . . a figure like the Son of Man." The passage is a description of Christ the Son of Man and not of the Father. Interestingly enough the imagery used to describe the Son of Man in Revelations is taken from the description of the Ancient of Days in Daniel. The use of the Ancient of Days imagery by St. John for the Son of Man in Revelations is nearly an open declaration of the identity of the two figures in the mind of the apostle.

The other vision in Revelations, 4:2-4, gives no anthropomorphic features to the "One who was sitting on the throne," but describes Him rather in terms of diamonds, emeralds, rubies, and rainbows. It seems clear that Christ is the subject of both visions for at the beginning of the second one, St. John says, "I . . . heard the same voice speaking to me. . . ." This statement makes it difficult to identify the One with the Father. The council's statement then seems to fall from nowhere, not even having a sound grounding in the biblical text itself. Even though it introduces an element of confusion and incoherence into the canon, the statement does not take away from the power of the canon itself as a statement of the mind of the Church.

Whatever ambiguity may have existed on the question

of the images of God the Father, as a result of the two previous Moscow councils, it seems now to have been cleared up. The Russian Church and the Church at large have a proper standard by which to judge the canonicity of so-called Trinity images.

The Stoglav Council of 1551 and the Great Council of Moscow 1666–67, stand together as beacons at a time when the Church was entering the darkest days of her western captivity. Even though the Council of 1553 serves as a counterpoint to the line of thinking represented by the other two councils, it serves as the exception that proves the rule. What Ostrogorsky says about the Stoglav Council, can equally be said about Moscow, 1666–67:

> Our studies have shown that the Stoglav Council introduced nothing new on the essence of the question but reflects and confirms the most ancient conceptions of iconography. Our studies also show that Stoglav faithfully reflects these conceptions, that it follows the principles of Byzantine iconography with perfect exactitude, that its decisions concerning the holy images, from the artistic as well as from the religious point of view are in intimate relation with the very essence of Orthodox beliefs and ideas, and that these decisions have their roots in those beliefs and ideas and flow directly from them.[99]

## 7: THE WESTERN ATTITUDE

An integral part of the thesis of this study is that the painting of images of God the Father in representations of the Trinity and elsewhere along with the theological justification of this practice are inspired by a mind other than that of the Orthodox Church concerning iconography. The attitude toward religious art found in western Latin Christianity, in our view, is at the base of this and other iconographic aberrations in the Orthodox Church. It is now our task to demonstrate this point. Our first task, then, is to show that two overlapping but different attitudes toward Church art exist in the two halves of Christianity. The attitudes are "overlapping" due to their common mind during the first millennium of Christian history and "different" due to a new mind developed in the Christian West during the second millennium. We can see these different attitudes beginning to show themselves as far back as the iconoclastic period itself, but they were to be brought into glaring contrast in the Western European Renaissance.

Speaking of the Byzantine argumentation during the second period of iconoclasm and especially of Theodore the Studite, Henri Leclercq says that

> images are not only a means of teaching when they acquaint us with the people and events of sacred history, but they also possess a miraculous value. They are the symbol of the Saints' victory over the demons and the most effective of all

protections against their traps. In images, something of their prototypes' intimate force and energy is found. Through them, the doors of the invisible and intelligible world open to us; through the intermediary of these sense signs, we are taken up in the spirit to their causes. . . .[100]

Still speaking of Theodore the Studite, Leclercq, quoting Bréhier, continues:

The Byzantine conception was thus hammered out in the ninth century. The image is a mystery which contains in itself divine energy and grace. It is logical therefore that the production of images cannot depend on the caprice of a painter or a sculptor. Nothing is left to chance: the type, the costume, the attitude of the persons, the composition of the scenes, all must conform to the tradition of the Church. The artist is not free to compose a painting anymore than a preacher is when he writes the text of his sermon. These are very narrow limits placed on the imagination of the artist.[101]

This mysterious, sacramental attitude of the Orthodox Church toward art is to be contrasted with another, western attitude already manifested during the iconoclastic period. The various reactions of western churchmen to Nicæa II and its theology can be attributed only in part to already well-studied causes: poor translations, cultural factors, political rivalries, temperament, etc. All of these factors being taken into account, an underlying mind of western Christianity toward religious art can already be seen and felt; it is present, for example, in the *Libri Carolini* published around 790 under the authority, if not the authorship, of the western emperor Charlemagne. The theology of Nicæa II is strongly criticized in these books:

If we sum up the main points about images set out in the *Libri Carolini,* we arrive at the following conclusions: . . . 4th) There are times when we give *adoratio* to men. This consists of bowing down in front of them or of kissing them, but we do that only through respect, love or humility. 5th) As for images, we ought not give this adoratio to them because they are lifeless and made by human hands. We should have them a) as ornaments in churches and b) as aids to recall ancient memories. We should not, however, give them adoratio or cultura.[102]

Now although the Pope was eventually able to have Nicæa II accepted by the whole of the West as an ecumenical council, its theology was never really understood or accepted and so never entered into the theological mind of the West concerning Church art.

This mind can be summarized in four categories of usefullness:[103] 1) Images instruct people about sacred events and people in the Scriptures and Church history. They are the Bible and history books of the illiterate according to the saying of St. Gregory Diagolos; they are pedagogical aides. 2) Images recall to memory the events and people represented; they are memory aids. 3) Images also inspire love, repentance, joy, etc. in the faithful, pious attitudes and feelings about the events and people depicted; they are inspirational tools. 4) Images beautify the churches with warm and pleasing forms and colors. It is more pleasing to enter a well decorated church than into one whose bare, perhaps stone, walls project a feeling of coldness; images are æsthetically pleasing objects.

These reasons based on usefulness are by no means rejected by the Orthodox mind on iconography. Many Fathers have mentioned them in various forms, and so eastern and western Christianity agree on these points. From the Orthodox point of view, however, western Christianity has never risen above such utilitarian reasons to the higher purpose of icons: the making present of the person represented, the entering into communion with that person in his transfigured humanity. The sacred image, the icon, shows us and draws us into that reality called the Kingdom of God. It is therefore perhaps more correct to describe the differences in attitudes between Orthodox and western Christianity as a partial sharing of approaches rather than as two totally opposed points of view. The West never went far enough, never went to the real heart of the question of images, their sacramental character. As a result, the actual artwork produced by the two halves of Christianity during the second millennium are evidently distinct. It is certain that individual western Christians have risen, and still do rise, to the level of sacramental appreciation of Church art, but by and large they have had little lasting influence.

> The first way in which the image can be useful for the Christian has already been mentioned above: it is the Bible of those who cannot read. . . . This pedagogical function is irreplaceable. . . . But it was in the West that this pedagogical role of the image was especially emphasized and developed, even to the detriment of its sacramental aspect.[104]

This is rather an understatement, and by a Roman Catholic writer too.

The ramifications of these two attitudes in the field of artworks are very great. If we believe that the purpose of Church art is essentially to educate, recall, inspire, and beautify, then we will be very open to the techniques, methods, temperament, mentality of the time and place in which we find ourselves. Taste will therefore be a very important factor in the production of Church art. The people to be instructed must be reached by the most effective methods possible. If they are very emotional, that element must appear in artwork if it is to appeal to them. If, on the other hand, a people is more reserved, that cultural characteristic will also be put into their Church art. The place of the artist is therefore very important since he is the one who translates a story, text, or idea into a visual presentation that will appeal to an audience. His talent and inspiration are central. Since he is called to illustrate a text or a story, his creativity in portraying it is of great significance. Between the sacred story and the artwork stands the artist, as a filtering or focusing agent. Except for certain general restraints of decency, propriety, and doctrine, the artist is quite free to illustrate a text or event as he sees fit. This latitude is seen as a great strength and virtue by the mind of western Christianity.

Contrast the artist's place in the western approach to that of the iconographer in the Orthodox tradition. He must have talent, of course, but of prime concern is his ability to translate into visual form what is prior to and greater than himself: the mind of the Church, the canon of iconography. The iconographer of necessity must himself have the mind and live the transfigured life in Christ that he is called on to portray in icons. His creativity, in the sense of unfettered ability to imagine and illustrate a text, event, or idea, is of little importance, and defined in this way, his creativity is to be repressed. The iconographer is not to show himself in his work and in the strictest tradition should not even be known. He is only the conveyance, the instrument to show something that he has already inherited, that is, the canonical tradition and the experience of transfiguration. To the degree that he passes on that tradition in his works, to that degree he will be successful. To the degree that he puts his own self into his work, in place of the tradition, to that degree, he will be a failure.

On the one hand, this ideal is strongly affirmed in the tradition, but on the other, we know that very concrete individual persons are iconographers, and so when they interpret the canonical tradition, fully desiring to follow it, they of necessity manifest those stylistic features which are part of their time and place and in so doing exercise their creativity. The depiction of horses, for example, will naturally reflect the iconographer's conception of a horse and the equipment of its rider. It is very easy to see the differences in time and place just from the way the canonical tradition is depicted. What is important, though, is that this stylistic element not become the primary reason for painting. Though a western Christian artist is quite free to abandon the past artistic tradition if he feels that it is ineffective and to blaze a new trail, such latitude is unthinkable for an iconographer. Though iconographers are subject to stylistic drift through time and place, the anchor of the canonical tradition makes them much less susceptible to its influence.

Let us now look at the question of images of God the Father in the light of the above. We have claimed, and hopefully shown, that the mind of the Orthodox Church and the patristic tradition are opposed to such images and that the Incarnation of the Word is the only basis for seeing and painting God. Furthermore, the Old Testament, in its prophecies and visions, was interpreted as a mine of obscure prefigurations of Christ. Is it possible now to demonstrate that theory from existing works of art along with any changes that may have taken place in the West? We think so.

Despite the various centrifugal forces at work in both eastern and western Christianity, it is commonplace to note that the East and West shared enough, including some basic points on art, to stay together for one thousand years. The fact that during this first millennium, we have no existing, direct images of God the Father or of the Trinity witnesses to a common mind, East and West.

> During the first centuries of Christianity, even as late as the twelfth century, no portraits of God the Father are to be seen. His presence is intimated only by a hand issuing from the clouds or from heaven.[105]

As noted in the chapter on the iconoclastic period, and again relevant here, there is no mention in all the iconoclastic controversy of any direct images of God the Father or the Trinity: the iconoclasts

> rose up against the images of Christ because, they said, to paint Jesus Christ, being God, would be to circumscribe the divinity. What would they have said, or what would they not have said, if along with images of Christ, Orthodox Christians also had images of God the Father or of the Holy Trinity? Nowhere do we encounter any objection or accusation on this subject.[106]

We can also see from art history that during this first millennium, it was Christ who was prefigured in the Old Testament. We have many examples where Christ is shown in scenes in which the Bible says God talked or showed himself to a prophet. We have in the following passage by the art historian Didron, in a peculiarly backhanded fashion, a witness to the patristic tradition. Didron is aware that for art history, it is the Son who is shown acting in scenes of the Old Testament, but he has a problem reconciling that with his preconceived idea that the Father is the actor, historically, as he puts it, in the Old Testament.

> Historically considered, the Father is the most frequently manifested in the Old Testament . . . while the Son is especially present in the Gospel and the Holy Ghost appears sometimes in one or sometimes in the other. In the Old Tes-

tament the Father reigns almost indivisible: He speaks, He shows Himself to man, acts, punishes, and rewards; He converses with Adam, Cain, Noah, Abraham, and Moses, with kings and prophets; He is with them in the midst of them; He is felt, seen, and heard everywhere; each verse speaks of Him.

Artists guided rather by history than by abstract and logical dogmas of theology understood Scripture in this literal sense at least at the end of the Gothic period; and in every scene of the Old Testament, God the Father is figured to the exclusion in some measure of the Son and the Holy Ghost. Still it was not til the end of the fourteenth century and primarily in the fifteenth and sixteenth, that God the Father was depicted by painters and sculptors.[107]

From the creed and from other theological sources, Didron knows that the Word was the active agent in the creation of the world, but he relegates theology to an almost irrelevant position and is continually astonished by the lack of direct depictions of God the Father in these scenes. We see that for Didron, and many other religious art historians, the patristic mind about the Old Testament typological prefigurations of Christ has long since been lost.

This typological approach, however, has been preserved in an iconographer's manual by Dionysius of Fourna, a manual based on earlier texts attributed to Manuel Panselinos of Mount Athos.[108] Dionysius prescribes that the Virgin and Child be painted in the middle of the burning bush which Moses saw on Mount Sinai. (*figs. 1 and 2*) We have here a double typology which Didron has even greater difficulty trying to understand.

> The Greeks not only substitute Christ for God the Father, but even the Virgin, and that too more than eleven hundred years before her birth.[109]

For the vision of Isaiah, Dionysius also prescribes that Christ be depicted.[110]

Fig. 1 Moses loosening the
sandals before the Virgin in the
Burning Bush.

Fig. 2 The Virgin of the
Burning Bush surrounded by
Moses, Aaron, Elijah, and Saint
Catherine.

Fig. 3 The Lord delivering the Law to Moses.

Fig. 4. Christ standing on the mountain, proclaiming the new Law.

Fig. 5. Christ with Adam and the Creation of Woman.

The loss of the sense of typology between the Old and the New Testaments has serious effects even in the realm of art history. As noted above, we have no representations of God the Father in the first millennium, but below it is claimed that there is such an image in late antiquity. However the scene described is quite normal and not of God the Father at all, but a typological representation of Christ.

> In Rome, in two lateral apses of the mausoleum of Saint Constantia, there are two compositions that were destined to become the most frequent themes of Christian art. In one, God the Father seated on the globe of the world gives Moses the Law; in the other, Christ standing on the mountain, from which flow mystical rivers, proclaims the new Law. He gives the text of this Law to St. Peter and its preaching to St. Paul.[111] *(figs. 3 and 4)*

On the other hand, the typological method of interpretation survived in the West even down to the era of the great Gothic cathedrals of the Middle Ages. We can still see there the common patristic mind of the Church put into plastic forms. At Chartres Cathedral, in the sculptures of the history of creation, Christ is represented thirteen times about thirty years old. *(For a twelfth century Sicilian example of the same theme, see fig. 5.)* He is also shown speaking to the prophet Elijah, and Rheims Cathedral has him speaking to Isaiah.[112]

As the Middle Ages wane in Western Europe, we arrive at a critical period; something revolutionary is about to take place. This revolution will affect many aspects of life and will also be reflected in art. This change of spirit is generally connected with the arrival of the Renaissance at various dates in various countries. In reference to our subject, the image of God the Father, we also see a dramatic break with the past and the mind of the Church: typology as a method of interpreting the scriptures is lost, God the Father is believed, "on historical grounds," to act and speak directly in the Old Testament, and direct depictions of him and the Trinity appear. This Renaissance spirit gives a great impetus to the free, interpretive creativity of the individual artist; this spirit is manifested in many ways in artworks, but most important for us, artists begin to paint portraits of the Trinity.

> In the fifteenth century and at the Renaissance more specifically, theological principles were losing their influence and at that period consequently, the Father is most frequently represented creating the world and not the Son or the Word. Besides, theology became at that time subordinate to history, and the incarnation of the Son of Man, being chronologically later than the creation, scruples seem to have arisen with regard to the propriety of representing him in that and similar subjects, and the Father was substituted in his place. Till at length, art grown bolder and more daring was not sorry to have an opportunity of attempting the imposing figure of Jehovah. . . .[113]

> The Middle Ages may therefore be divided into two periods with reference to God the Father. In the first, anterior to the fourteenth century, the figure of the Father is confounded with that of the Son: the Son is treated as all powerful and the Father is invested with his image and likeness. In the second period extending after the thirteenth down to the sixteenthth century, Christ loses his ascendancy in iconographic assimilation, he succumbs to the Father whose form he in his turn assumes and becomes like him aged and wrinkled.[114]

We have, then, on the modern side of this great watershed in art history and theology, all the elements that characterize the western attitude toward Church art and of course all the elements which separate it from the continuing Orthodox mind: Church art as pedagogy, as inspiration, as memory aids and as æsthetic objects. These elements were allied with the new freedom from theological guidance, emphasizing individual artistic creativity. Although Didron, below, speaks with some pride and eloquence of western Christian religious art being able to rise to meet a great challenge, his presentation could not be a more perfect statement of how far, from the point of view of Orthodox iconographic principles, the West had drifted from its own biblical and patristic roots.

> [Western] Christian art would not have shrunk from the task of creating a visible form as the interpretation or symbol of an invisible substance; such a theme presented on the contrary a magnificent opportunity for the exercise of its glowing imagination in investing with materiality the most elevated, the most sublime of all existing ideas, in clothing the divinity with form and substance. Such a theme would unquestionably have been appropriated by the art with joyous alacrity ever ready as it has been to give a body to impalpable ideas and to invest with life so many visionary and metaphysical abstractions.[115]

What is sad about Didron's observation is not so much his statement that God the Father is a "visionary and metaphysical abstraction," but that he does not seem to realize that God has already done in Christ what Didron is calling on art to do: create "a visible form . . . of an invisible substance, . . . clothing the divinity with form and substance."

Although this new attitude in Western Europe became well established, the Roman Catholic Church was by no means indifferent to art and the individual creations of artists, whose services were eagerly sought after and whose creations were highly prized. But only when certain artists went beyond the already very flexible limits did Church authorities react. Certain representations of the Trinity were condemned. Images of God as a three-headed man, for example, were condemned by the

Council of Trent and branded as heretical by Pope Urban VIII, who had them burned.[116] Any image of the Trinity that lent itself to the idea of tritheism, such as the picture of three men sitting on thrones, was also forbidden. What we have here is the illustrative principle at work: How well does this piece of art express the theological idea of the Trinity, three in one and one in three. If either side of the equation receives too much attention thus obscuring the other, then it could lead people into heresy and so should be condemned.

The Roman Catholic Church also had to contend with attacks on the very idea of representing God the Father at all, from within and from without. The iconoclastic tendencies of the Reformers are well known, and among other things, they attacked images of the Trinity.

> These images of the Trinity provoked ironic sarcasm from the Protestants. Pierre Dumoulin wrote in his *Bouclier de la foi* [Shield of the Faith]: "The temples of the Roman Church are full of images of the Trinity. They paint an old man seated on a throne dressed as the pope with a triple crown and the papal mantle so that at least the old man will be respected because of his habit. They also paint on him a pigeon hanging from his beard and a crucifix between his arms."[117]

On this point, the Roman Catholic Church defended itself by adopting its basic position on such images, set out at the Council of Trent.

> If sometimes paintings of stories taken from Holy Scripture are made in the judgment that these are useful for the instruction of the simple people, those in authority will take care to let the people know that we do not claim at all by such paintings to represent the Divinity, as if it could be seen with our bodily eyes or expressed by lines and colors.[118]

While, on the one hand, direct images of God the Father were defended against Protestant attacks of their total impropriety, on the other, a certain reserve was felt about them, such that they were permitted but not really encouraged.

> As for images of God which represent him in the form that he appeared in the Old and the New Testament, they are only permitted and following the commentaries of Bossuet, "these paintings should be rare according to the intention of the council which has left the decision to retain them or to suppress them to the discretion of the bishops. . . ."[119]

Open attacks also came from within the Roman Catholic Church. They provoked three separate papal reactions, all, of course, in conformity with the Council of Trent's framework of permitting but not encouraging images of God the Father and direct depictions of the Trinity.

1. The Baianists and the Jansenists declared that representations of God the Father should not be in the churches. This was the 25th of 31 propositions condemned by Alexander VIII, August 24, 1690. (Denzinger-Bannwart, *Enchiridion* n. 1315, voir t. I col. 759–760).[120]

2. In 1745, Benedict XIV confirmed the condemnation of the three-headed Trinity and gave official sanction to the image of the Trinity called the Throne of Grace:

   Representations of the Most Holy Trinity are generally approved and safely to be permitted which portray the Person of God the Father in the form of an old man taken from Daniel 7:9: the Ancient of Days; and in his lap his only begotten Son Christ, God and Man; between each of them the Paraclete, the Holy Spirit in the form of a dove.[121]

3. In 1786, the Council of Pistoia proposed to remove all the images of the Trinity from the churches because they were the occasion of heresy for the faithful. In the bull *Auctorem fidei*, Pius VI condemned the council's proposition as contrary to the usage of the Church and the piety of the faithful.[122]

On the basis of these three papal pronouncements as well as the declaration of the Council of Trent, we have a picture of the official Roman Catholic position regarding images of God the Father and the Trinity. They

1. are permitted though not encouraged;

2. have been sanctioned by the usage of the Church;

3. are justified on the belief that the Father appeared to the prophets in the Old Testament, especially to Daniel as the Ancient of Days.

Comparing this picture with the older biblical and patristic view of the Orthodox Church, the reaction of Pierre Miquel is an understatement to say the least:

> If the magisterium of the [Roman] Church rejects the prohibition of representations of the Father or of the Trinity, it remains that these images are theologically disputable.[123]

This Roman Catholic attitude toward images of God the Father is part of what Ouspensky is talking about when he speaks of Catholic and Protestant influence leading to the western captivity of Orthodoxy.

> Despite the vigorous opposition of the Church, there began the penetration not merely of separate elements but of the very principles of western religious art which are alien to Orthodoxy.[124]

We have already seen in the chapter on the three Russian councils that this western influence did not enter unnoticed or unprotested. Patriarch Nikon of Moscow (1652–1658) used to have western style icons destroyed and threatened to excommunicate those who painted or kept them. Patriarch Joachim of Moscow (1679–1690) also fought against German and Latin style images, saying that they were invented by the personal whim (otherwise known as "artistic creativity") of the artists, and were corrupting the Church. In the Greek-speaking world as far back as the fifteenth century, St. Simeon of Thessalonica vigorously protested the naturalistic and untraditional elements creeping into the painting of icons.[125]

The infiltration of western attitudes toward art along with direct borrowings can clearly be seen in the previously mentioned painter's manual of Dionysius of Fourna. We can see the general influence of the West in that many of the scenes prescribed for the iconographer are taken from known western sources: 1) The Lamentation at the Tomb and the Entombment of Christ rely heavily on Bonaventure's thirteenth century *Meditationes*.[126] 2) The imagery of the Parable of the Houses Built on Rock and Sand is very closely related to late, western medieval images of the Temptation of St. Anthony.[127] 3) There are two scenes for depicting the Holy Liturgy: one late and developed showing God the Father and the other, the traditional and canonical depiction of Christ giving communion.[128] 4) The scenes from Revelations are based on 22 woodcuts published in an illustrated New Testament in 1523 by Holbein; God the Father is depicted many times in this section.[129] 5) There are also definite western models behind "How the Second Coming of Christ is Represented."[130] 6) The Christmas icon: "A cave, with inside it on the right the Mother of God kneeling and laying the infant Christ, wrapped in swaddling clothes, in the crib; on the left Joseph is kneeling with his hands crossed on his breast."[131]

We have earlier seen that Dionysius preserves some of the typological interpretations of Old Testament visions and prophecies. Alongside the older canonical tradition, however, we have God the Father depicted in the creation of Adam and Eve.[132] In the section 'Titles for the

Holy Trinity,' the "Eternal Father" is also called the "Ancient of Days."[133] The most interesting blending of the canonical and western traditions is seen in a theological section on "Whence we derive the practice of painting images and worshiping [*sic!!*] them."

> The painting of holy images we take over not only from the holy fathers, but also from the holy Apostles and even from the person of Christ our only God. . . . We therefore depict Christ on an icon as a man, since he came into the world and had dealings with men, becoming in the end a man like us except in sin. Likewise we also depict the Timeless Father as an old man, as Daniel saw him clearly. . . .[134]

In an otherwise very well stated Orthodox position on iconography, we have in one small sentence, sixteen words, the tip of the iceberg of the western attitude toward religious art: a concise resumé of the position defended by Metropolitan Makary and Benedict XIV.

## 8: THE EVIDENCE OF ART HISTORY

 In this chapter we refer to some specific artworks related to our study to see what light they may shed on the question of images of God the Father. It was claimed in the last chapter that there are no examples of direct representations of the Father or the Trinity during the first millennium of Christian history. This artistic void is used to support the claim that the mind of the Church in the East and the West would not have permitted such a thing. There is, supposedly, one exception to this claim. In the Lateran Museums in Rome, there is a Christian sarcophagus (*figs. 6 and 7*) which shows the creation of Adam and Eve. The three men presiding over the creation are, according to André Grabar, an early attempt to represent the Trinity.[135] Walter Lowrie agrees with this interpretation and assigns the sarcophagus to the fourth or fifth century.[136] If, in the second scene, as Lowrie claims, it is Christ who is giving Adam and Eve their respective labors, of farming and spinning, then in addition to being a piece of counter-evidence to our thesis and Didron's claim that there is no image of God the Father in the first millennium, this sarcophagus also provides us with an example, at a very early date, of the typological method of interpreting the Old Testament.

Assuming that this sarcophagus is an attempt at a di-

Fig. 6. Christian sarcophagus showing the creation of Adam and Eve, upper left-hand corner.

Fig. 7. Christian sarcophagus showing the creation of Adam and Eve, enlargement of the upper left-hand corner of figure 6.

rect representation of God the Father and the Trinity, why is there only one such example? If one artist thought to create such an image, why not others?

> The fact that this sarcophagus in the Lateran Museums is unique plainly indicates its lack of success, since the workshops that produced sarcophagi tended to repeat everything they had learned to represent. But here, by exception, we find only once the attempt to represent the Trinity by showing three identical Persons.... The failure of such a figuration is understandable, since it retains only the idea of the identity of the three divine Persons, entirely neglecting their unity.[137]

We might suggest rather that the reason this model failed to take root is not so much related to an imbalance in the representation of two abstract ideas, "threeness in oneness" and "oneness in threeness," but rather because the mind of the Church could not allow such an aberration to grow and develop. The theological environment in which this seed germinated was so hostile as not to allow the plant to survive.

We ought not to be greatly surprised or to allow this one example to demolish the thesis defended in this study. We know that there have been doubtful opinions put forth by many people on various subjects before the mind of the Church was set out on such and such a question. We can look at this sarcophagus as a parallel phenomenon on the artistic level. What is important is not that some artists – only one as far as we really know – produced one piece of aberrant art during one thousand years. What is significant is that such creations were not accepted.

André Grabar describes other attempts to symbolically represent the Trinity during Christianity's first millennium. The following are some of those attempts:[138]

Fig. 8. *The eagle image of the Trinity as found on a wall painting in Bawait, Egypt.*

Fig. 9. *The Hand of God (the Father) combined with a dove and Christ at the Ascension.*

Fig. 10. *The Hand of God (the Father) combined with a dove and Christ at the Baptism.*

1. A fresco in Bawit, Egypt, showing three wreaths on a Roman imperial eagle. (fig. 8)

2. The Hand of God (the Father) combined with a dove and Christ at the Ascension or the Baptism. (figs. 9 and 10)

3. The Magi used for representing the Trinity, a theme based on early Semitic legends that attribute special visions to the Magi. In this connection, Grabar claims that this legend is reflected in an eleventh century miniature from Constantinople (*Taphon, Codex 14*, Jerusalem: Greek Patriarchal Library) in which the Trinity is represented, each of the magi carrying a Person: the Ancient of Days as God the Father; Christ; the Child Emmanuel representing the Holy Spirit.

There are some problems with this interpretation, however. First of all there is no tradition in which Emmanuel has ever symbolized the Holy Spirit. Secondly, the whole composition is only assumed to represent the Trinity because the Ancient of Days is supposed to be God the Father. If we suppose that the Church's typological consciousness was still strong in eleventh century Constantinople – there is no reason to suppose it was not – then the Ancient of Days is to be interpreted as a symbol of Christ. The whole representation, therefore, is not trinitarian at all but a triple representation of Christ. This seems very reasonable since the Magi are intimately related to the Christmas story and the Incarnation itself. The same arrangement of images is seen in an eleventh century Byzantine gospel book. (fig. 11) Another gospel shows only the Ancient of Days as a prototype of Christ. (fig. 12) The fact that these images appear on

Fig. 11. An eleventh-century Byzantine gospel book showing a triple representation of Christ.

Fig. 12. A gospel book showing the Ancient of Days as a prototype of Christ.

Fig. 13. *The Throne of God as a Trinitarian image.*

Fig. 14. *The Throne of God as a Trinitarian image.*

Fig 15. The Throne of God.

gospel books strengthens the connection with Christ and helps set aside any trinitarian interpretation. A quasi-trinitarian misinterpretation is adopted by the Bibliothèque Nationale, Paris, in describing the first of the two above-mentioned gospel books. Its miniatures are explained as "St John; the following figures are shown in the three lower medals: in the center (*o palaios emerai*); at the right and left, a double image of Christ (*Iesous Xristos and Emmanuel*)".[139] At least there is no attempt to make Emmanuel into a symbol of the Holy Spirit. Again we see that not having as one's own the theological mind that produced many ancient Christian works of art, or at least not being aware of it, has serious consequences for the interpretation of these artworks.

4. The cross or lamb, dove, and hand of God (the Father) from *Epistula XXXII* of St. Paulinus of Nola to Severus describing such images used in a cluster.

5. An empty throne, a dove, a cross or gospel book. (*figs. 13 and 14. For two relatively modern examples, circa 1450 and 1573 from Mt. Sinai, see figs. 15 and 16.*)

6. The Hospitality of Abraham.

As we can see, all these attempts are either symbolic representations of the Trinity or images of Christ and not trinitarian at all. Although art history cannot prove or disprove the claim that there is a mind of the Church about iconography which prohibited direct depictions of the Father or the Trinity in the first Christian millennium, it firmly establishes the fact that, with one possible exception, there are no direct images of the Father. There may, of course, be other interpretations to explain the void, but our thesis at least stands the test of

Fig. 16. The Throne of God.

the evidence of art history.

Let us now move to the period when direct images of God the Father and the Trinity begin to appear and are reproduced. Excluding the sarcophagus mentioned above, there seems to be general agreement about the first extant, direct depiction of the Trinity. It is found in an early eleventh century Greek manuscript of the Vatican Library (ms gr 394, fol. 7) containing an illustrated text of The Heavenly Ladder of St. John Climacus. (figs. 17 and 18) This image shows an old man holding a child in his lap and a dove in the lap of the child. The image is entitled in Greek "The Ancient of Days Jesus Christ." There seems to be some disagreement among art historians as to whether there is in fact a dove in the child's lap. Heimann[140] and Martin[141] say there is a dove and Papadopoulos[142] and Gerstinger[143] claim the opposite. It appears, however, that on close examination there is a dove. Heimann has a very odd comment about the description of the image, and it may throw some light on other aspects of her interpretation. She says erroneously that this image is the most adequate one for the Trinity because it conforms to the Orthodox faith which says that the Holy Spirit proceeds only from the Son.[144] She also claims that this image is of Byzantine origin.

There is a controversy among certain art historians about the origin of this model of the Trinity. Is it Byzantine or western (French) in origin? Réau[145] and Emile Mâle[146] argue that it is western and French while Heimann and Leroquais[147] claim a Byzantine origin. Gerstinger proposes western models influenced possibly by Byzantine images of the Virgin Nikopoia.[148] Also, what is meant by "Byzantine origin"? Gerstinger proposes two kinds: Italo-Byzantine and Byzantino-Slav.[149] We would need to be careful of any Byzantine origins in

*Fig. 17. Direct depiction of the Trinity: An old man holding a child in his lap and a dove in the lap of the child.*

*Fig. 18. Direct depiction of the Trinity: An old man holding a child in his lap and a dove in the lap of the child.*

*Fig. 19. Early direct depiction of God the Father in the Trinity on a Greek manuscript of the Gospels.*

southern Italy. Due to the heavy westernizing influence there, the authenticity of its "Byzantineness" may be suspect. As the Middle Ages advance, the Byzantine character of southern Italy will become just an historical memory.

It would fit in well with the thesis of our study if it were shown that this model of the Trinity, called *Paternitas* or *otechestvo*, were of purely western origins or at least Italo-Byzantine. However, if it is of Byzantino-Slav origin, we would simply note, as in the case of the fourth or fifth century sarcophagus, that it is very rare; it is one example in an illuminated manuscript, but as a model it had little influence in Orthodox Byzantine areas until their theological soil had been altered by later importations of western attitudes so as to allow for a more luxuriant growth. Again what is significant by contrast is not the existence of this image or its possible Byzantine origins, but how it is adopted and widely and deeply developed by the medieval Christian West.

A second example of a very early direct depiction of God the Father in the Trinity is found in another Greek manuscript of the gospels: Vienna Library *(Cod supl. gr 52 fol. I verso)*.[150] *(figs. 19 and 20)* It is dated from about 1150 and was done in a Greek monastery in Italy.[151] Still another early image of the Trinity similar to the second was discovered in 1904 in the Greek monastery of Grottaferrata near Rome. The fresco itself is dated at between 1250–1300.[152] *(fig. 21)*

Below are other early representations of the Trinity:[153]

1. *The Jerusalem Psalter, Taphos Ms 53 fol. 162* illustrating psalm 109. Note that in this Greek psalter God the Father is not represented directly but implied by an empty throne, 1050 A.D. *(fig. 22)*

Fig. 20. Early direct depiction of God the Father in the Trinity on a Greek manuscript of the Gospels.

Fig. 21. Fresco in the Greek monastery of Grottaferrata near Rome. (circa 1250-1300)

*Fig. 22. The Jerusalem Psalter: the empty throne.*

*Fig. 23. The Utrect Psalter: The "binity".*

*Fig. 24. The Offices of New Minister, Winchester: a "quinity".*

Fig. 25 The Harley Ms 603 fol.1: a clear Trinity.

Fig. 26. The Canterbury Psalter: a "binity".

Fig. 27. Ivory Seal of Godwin. illustrating psalm 109, eleventh century.

2. *The Utrecht Psalter,* early 1000's showing a "binity," again from Psalm 109: "The Lord said to my lord. . . ." *(fig. 23)*

3. *The Offices of New Minster,* Winchester, illustrating the office for Trinity Sunday: a "quinity," 1020 A.D. *(fig. 24)*

4. *The Harley Ms 603 fol. 1:* a clear Trinity, early eleventh century. *(fig. 25)*

5. *The Canterbury Psalter,* again a "binity" illustrating Psalm 109, twelfth century. *(fig. 26)*

6. *Ivory Seal of Godwin,* illustrating psalm 109, eleventh century. *(fig. 27)*

7. Fresco in the monastery church at Ravanica, Serbia, fourteenth century: Crucifixion scene with God the Father above and dove between Him and Christ.[154] *(fig. 28)*

8. Fresco in St. George's church near the monastery of Preveli, Crete, 1462 A.D., shows God the Father holding Emmanuel with a dove coming out of the mouth of the Father. Perhaps this is an attempt to produce an "Orthodox" image to counter the Roman Catholic doctrine of the filioque.[155] *(fig. 29)* Kantorowicz claims that the oldest western anthropomorphic images of the Trinity go back to England beginning with the eleventh century, but agrees with Heimann about the eastern or Byzantine origin of the model of three identical men or of two men and a dove.[156]

The rest of the images of the Trinity which the various art historians deal with are all variations of this model, *Paternitas,* as well as of models that have unquestioned western origins. The only model that art

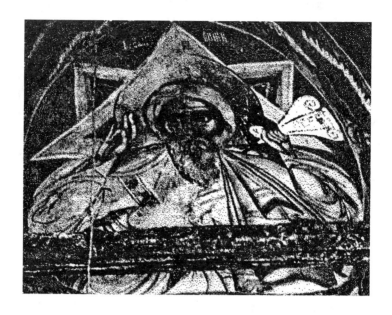

*Figs. 28 & 28a. God the Father above and dove between Him and Christ in Crucifixion below. (Fresco in the monastery church at Ravanica, Serbia, fourteenth century.)*

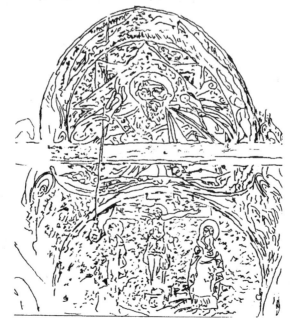

*Fig. 29. God the Father holding Emmanuel with a dove coming out of the mouth of the Father (Fresco at St. George's Church near the monastery of Preveli, Crete, 1462 A.D.).*

historians can solidly show to be of Byzantine origin and to have taken deep roots in Orthodox Byzantine areas is the Hospitality of Abraham.

> In any case, this model [*Paternitas*] is alien to Orthodox dogmatics which only knows the symbolic representation of the Hospitality of Abraham.[157]

Hopefully, what we have shown up to this point makes clear why this symbolic image of the Trinity is so widespread and deeply rooted in Orthodox areas and further why up to the time of known western influence in these areas, direct depictions of God the Father in the Trinity are relatively unknown: the Hospitality of Abraham is the only image of the Trinity which accords with the Church's mind on iconography.

## 9. CONCLUSION

Throughout this study, we have claimed that any representation of God the Father presenting itself as a portrait icon is forbidden in Orthodox iconology. An icon is a means of seeing a person in his circumscribed human nature. In reference to seeing God in a portrait icon, it is the Orthodox belief that we see God only in the Incarnation of the Word, Jesus Christ, and to paint an icon of Him is to see His person in His circumscribed human nature which He took from the Theotokos. He cannot be seen, nor can we paint Him, in His divine nature, since He is uncircumscribed and therefore inaccessible to our perception in any direct way. We have icons of the saints based on the same principle of seeing persons painted in their transfigured human natures.

The Church has consistently permitted the painting of angels on the basis of showing their persons symbolized in the human form in which they have from time to time appeared to men. We have here a modification of the principle of painting a person in a human nature because, though an angel does not have a human nature, his person is symbolized in and by a human form. This kind of representation is permitted on the grounds that an angelic nature is circumscribed; angels are created, limited beings. Painting them in symbolic human form stretches but does not destroy the principle depicting of a person in a human nature. The image of visible, circumscribed humanity is borrowed to depict the invisible, though equally circumscribed, angelic world.

A second principle is here introduced into Orthodox iconology: symbolism. According to this principle one thing represents (stands in for, takes the place of, refers our minds to, etc.) another thing which has a different nature from what is represented: a lamb represents Christ, a burning bush the Theotokos, the Theotokos the Church, an egg Pascha, a throne the bishop, etc. The terms type and prototype, symbol, symbolized, figure and fulfillment, image, allegory, and others have been used to characterize the relation of the thing seen and the thing unseen but called to memory. Sometimes a person is used to represent another person, such as an ambassador for a king, but that is rare. What a symbol does not do, however, in contrast to an icon, is show the actual person, so that, in seeing the symbol, we can say that we have seen the person. An icon answers the question, "Who is that?". A symbol answers the question, "Who or what does that stand for?".

Now the question comes up: Is it possible to symbolize God the Father, and if so, how? Everyone agrees that we cannot paint His person in His divine nature, but can we represent His person symbolized in some other nature? In other words, can we combine the two principles of iconology (person-in-human-nature and symbolism) to represent God the Father? No. Angelic persons are, by stretching the first principle, representable in human form only because human *and* angelic natures are circumscribed. Such representations of angelic persons are therefore strictly exceptional. We cannot extend that principle to God the Father by showing His person in a circumscribed nature when His is an uncircumscribed one. To do this would be to separate His person and nature in a way foreign to Orthodox dogmatics. It would imply that we can have and show a person extracted from His nature and, vice-versa, a nature not concretized in a person. The trinitarian and christological debates of the early Church centered around the relation of nature and person. The conclusion was that nature does not exist outside its concretization in a person; nor can a person exist outside his nature. The two are distinguishable but not separable. Clearly a representation which claims to show, as in a portrait icon, a person not in his nature would imply an unacceptable separation of the two. This is all the more true when we consider God the Father since we would be showing His person in a circumscribed nature.

There is, then, only one principle left, the symbolic, whereby the person is not shown but rather represented by something of a totally different nature. This symbol makes us think of God the Father but does not show His person in His divine or any other pretended nature: for example, an empty throne, the space between the two cherubim on the ark of the Covenant, a circle of light at the Baptism of Christ, an angel. This is in fact the level of representation that is preserved in Orthodox iconology by permitting the Hospitality of Abraham to symbolize the Holy Trinity and God the Father.

We have seen that late western theology and iconography, having lost the typological mind and method of interpreting the Scriptures, took the shadowy Old Testament prefigurations of Christ, primarily the Ancient of Days, and used them to represent the Father on the principle of symbolizing or showing His person without depicting His nature. Such theology and iconography is quite alien to the Orthodox mind. Any iconology which defends such representation of God the Father is unfortunately grounded in another mind than that of the Orthodox Church. The impression is often given that Orthodox Christians, having unknowingly absorbed parts of the western mind and finding themselves criticized for painting God the Father in direct depictions of the Trinity, needed to present a defense and naturally adopted the only defense available: that of those who produced and developed these images in the first place, that is, medieval and tridentine Roman Catholics. Orthodox Christians like Metropolitan Makary, knowing that Holy Tradition was a determining factor in dogmatic considerations, believed or were convinced that such images had been sanctioned by the use of the Church. We in fact know otherwise.

In our time, when the Orthodox Christianity is waking up to the sad state of her colonization by western Christian forms and ideas, it is particularly important for all of us, as guardians of Holy Tradition, to insure that the iconographic expression of the Church's mind is restored and promoted. Happily such oversight is being exercised in the form of committees and associations whose task it is to study and supervise iconography in the Church. Even though we in this fallen world are always confronted with mixtures of good and evil, purity and impurity, transfiguration and corruption, etc., there are limits below which we cannot allow ourselves to sink: permitting and defending direct images of God the Father, alone or in so-called New Testament Trinities, is a deformation of Holy Tradition that we must strive to eliminate.

# NOTES

1  For a full treatment of this subject see, George A. Barrois, *The Face of Christ in the Old Testament*, St. Vladimir's, Crestwood, N. Y., 1974.

2  *Epistle to Polycarp*, III, *The Ante-Nicene Fathers*, 1 (hereafter cited as ANF), Eerdmans, Grand Rapids, Mich., 1979, p. 94.

3  *Dialogue with Trypho*, ch. 128 and 56, ANF, I, p. 264 and pp. 222-25 respectively.

4  *Ibid.*, ch. 60, p. 227.

5  J.N.D. Kelly, *Early Christian Doctrine*, Adam and Charles Black, London, 1975, p. 99.

6  *Against Heresies*, IV, IX, 1, ANF, I, p. 472.

7  *Ibid.*, V, XVI, 2, p. 544.      8  *Ibid.*, IV, XX, 9, p. 490.

9  *Ibid.*, IV, XX, 9-11, pp. 490-91.      10  *Ibid.*, IV, VI, 6, p. 469.

11  *Adversus Praxeas* 16, cited in Henry Bettenson, *The Early Christian Fathers*, Oxford University Press, London, 1963, p. 167.

12  *The Second Theological Oration*, Oration XXVIII, ch. III, *The Nicene and Post-Nicene Fathers*, 7, Eerdmans, Grand Rapids, 1979, p. 289.

13  *Ibid.*, ch. IV, p. 289.      14  *Ibid.*, ch. VII, p. 290.

15  *Ibid.*, ch. XVIII, p. 295.      16  *Ibid.*, ch. XIX, p. 295.

17  Vladimir Lossky, *The Vision of God*, The Faith Press, Clayton, Wisconsin, 1963, p. 77.

18  Christoph Von Schonborn, *L'icône du Christ: fondement théologiques*, Editions Universitaires, Fribourg, Switzerland, 1976, pp. 64-5. Eusebius cited from *Demonstratio Evangelica*, 9, 7.

19  Kelly, p. 273.

20  Pierre Miquel, "Culte des Images," *Dictionnaire de Spiritualité*, Fas. XLVIII-XLIX (hereafter cited as DS) Beauchesne, Paris, 1970, pp. 1515-16.

21  *Commentary on Daniel*, PG, 81, 1321-25 (English translation by Lambros Kamperidis, Montreal, PQ).

22  *Vision 12: Œuvres spirituelles*, E. des Places, tr., Sources chrétiennes, 5, 1966, p. 172. Cited in Lossky, p. 96.

23  V. Grumel, "Images (Culte Des)" *Dictionnaire de Théologie Catholique*, 7, 1, Letouzey et Ané, Paris, 1927, p. 838, (here-

after cited as DTC).

24 For a full consideration of this canon see Leonid Ouspensky, *The Theology of the Icon*, "The Qunisext Council: Its Teaching on the Icon," St. Vladimir's, 1978, pp. 113-124. For a later edition of this same chapter see Ouspensky, *La Théologie de l'icône dans l'Eglise orthodoxe*, "Le concile quinisexte et son enseignement sur l'image sacrée," Cerf, Paris, 1980, pp. 71-81.

25 *The Seven Ecumenical Councils, The Nicene and Post-Nicene Fathers*, Eerdmans, Grand Rapids, 1979, p. 401.

26 ' V. Grumel, "L'Iconologie de Saint Germain de Constantinople," *Echos d'Orient*, 21, 1922, pp. 165-75.

27 DTC, p. 838.

28 For a consideration of their authenticity, see J. Gouillard, "Grégoire II et l'Iconoclasme," *Travaux et Mémoires*, Centre de Recherche d'histoire et civilisation byzantines, III, Paris, 1968.

29 C. J. Hefele, *A History of the Councils of the Church*, 626-787, 5, Clark, Edinburgh, 1896, p. 291.

30 *Ibid.*

31 St. John of Damascus, *On the Divine Images*, David Anderson, tr., St. Vladimir's, 1980, p. 18.

32 *Ibid.*, p. 23. For notes 33–46, only the page numbers will be given for *On the Divine Images*.

33 p. 52.   34 p. 58.   35 p. 87.   36 p. 20.

37 p. 34.   38 p. 36.   39 p. 40.   40 pp. 20-1.

41 p. 80.   42 p. 30.   43 p. 41.   44 pp. 78-9.

45 p. 65.   46 p. 16.   47 DTC, p. 839.

48 St. Theodore the Studite, *On the Holy Icons*, St. Vladimir's, Crestwood, 1981, p. 82.

49 *Ibid.* p. 21. For notes 50–55, only the page numbers will be given for *On the Holy Icons*.

50 p. 81.   51 p. 92.   52 pp. 100-1. 53 pp. 88-9.

54 p. 64.   55 p. 25.

56 J. Gouillard, "Le Synodikon de l'Orthodoxie: Edition et Textes," *Travaux et Mémoires*, Centre de Recherche d'histoire et civilisation byzantines, 2, Paris, 1967, p. 50.

57 *Ibid.*

58 M. Jugie, "Constantinople (IVe Concile de)," DTC, III, 1908, p. 1297.

59 Thomas Hopko, *The Orthodox Faith*, I: Doctrine, The Department of Religious Education: The Orthodox Church in America, New York, 1981, p. 19.

60 *The Festal Menaion* (hereafter cited as FM), Mother Mary and Archimandrite Kallistos Ware, trs., Faber, London, 1969, p. 263.

61 *Le Triode de Carême*, 1 (hereafter cited as TC#1; tomes 2 and 3 of the same work will be cited as TC#2 and TC#3), P. Denis Guillaume, tr. Collège Grec de Rome, Rome, 1978, p. 301.

62 TC#1, p. 17.          63 TC#3, p. 70.

64 Ouspensky, p. 180.

65 FM, p. 215.          66 FM, p. 301.

67 *Le Pentecostaire*, 1 (hereafter cited as P#1; tome 2 of this same work will be cited as P#2), p. Denis Guillaume, tr. Collège Grec de Rome, Rome, 1978, p. 119.

68 FM, p. 476.     69 FM, p. 408.     70 FM, pp. 115-6.

71 FM, p. 216.     72 FM, p. 413.     73 FM,p.415.

74 FM, p. 418.     75 FM, pp. 420-1.  76 FM, p. 422.

77 TC#2, p. 322.   78 FM, p. 15.      79 FM, p. 180.

80 FM, p. 205.     81 FM, p. 422.     82 FM, p. 298.

83 FM, p. 301.     84 TC#1, p. 303.   85 TC#1, p. 281.

86 *Euchologe ou rituel de l'Eglise orthodoxe*, Archimandrite Alexandre Nelidow and Antoine Nivière trs., Paix, Le Bousquet d'Orb, France, 1979, pp. 178-84; see also the Slavonic version of the texts, *Trebnik*, The Holy Synod of the Russian Orthodox Church, Moscow, 1911.

87 E. Duchesne, *Le Stoglav ou les Cent chapitres: Recueil des Décisions de l'Assemblée Ecclésiastique de Moscou, 1551*, Bibliothèque de l'Institut Français de Petrograd, 5, Librairie Ancienne Honoré Champion, Ed., Paris, 1920, p. 28.

88 *Ibid.*, p. 111.     89 *Ibid.*, p. 112.     90 *Ibid.*, p. 133.

91 *Ibid.*, p. 135.     92 *Ibid.*, p. 136.

93 Georg Ostrogorsky, "Les Décisions du 'Stoglav' Concernant la Peinture d'Images et les Principes de l'Iconographie Byzantine," *Byzanz und Die Welt Der Slawen, Wissenschaftliche Buchgesellschaft*, Darmstadt, 1974, p. 130.

94 *Ibid.*     95 *Ibid.*, p. 131     96 *Ibid.*

97 *Acts of the Moscow Council of 1666-67*, The Holy Synod of the Russian Church, 1893, pp. 22-24, English translation by Alexander L. Dvorkin, St. Vladimir's Seminary, November,

1981. For a French translation of this same text and a consideration of the entire council see Ouspensky, *La Théologie de l'icône*, chp. XV, "Le Grand Concile de Moscou et l'image de Dieu le Père," pp. 345-386.

98  Ouspensky, p. 360.       99  Ostrogorsky, p. 140.

100 Henri Leclercq, "Images (Culte et Querelle des)," *Dictionnaire d'Archéologie chrétienne et de Liturgie* (hereafter cited as DACL) 7,1, Librairie Letouzey et Ané, Paris, 1920, p. 273.

101 Louis Bréhier, *L'Art chrétien: son développement iconographique des origines à nos jours*, Paris, 1918, pp. 125-26, quoted in Leclercq DACL, col. 273-274.

102 *Ibid.*, p. 270.  103 DTC, pp. 797-800  104 DS, p. 1516.

105 M. Didron, *Christian Iconography*, I, E. J. Millington, tr., London, 1851, p. 201.

106 DTC, p. 839.       107 Didron, pp. 167-69.

108 On the Dating of Panselinos, see *The Painter's Manual of Dionysius of Fourna*, Paul Hetherington, tr., Oakwood Publications, Torrance, CA, 1989, note 2 for page 2 in back, p. 91.

109 Didron, p. 172.       110 Dionysius, pp. 21 and 24.

111 DACL, p. 202.       112 Didron, pp. 175 and 177.

113 *Ibid.*, p. 196  114 *Ibid.*, p. 220.  115 *Ibid.*, p. 200.

116 Louis Réau, *Iconographie de l'art chrétien, II: Iconographie de la Bible, I, Ancien Testament*, Presses Universitaires de France, 1956, p. 22.

117 *Ibid.*, p. 27.

118 *Le Saint Concile de Trente*, tr., 2, Session 25, M. L'Abbé Dassance,"De l'Invocation de la Vénération et des Reliques, des Saints et des Saintes Images," Paris, 1842, p. 293.

119 DTC, p. 812, cited from Bossuet, *Culte des Images*, I, *Œuvres complètes*, Bloud et Barral, III, *Controverse*, p. 71, cited from *Dictionnaire de Théologie Catholique*, 7, 1. Paris: Librairie Letouzey et Ané, 1927.

120 *Ibid.*, p. 785.

121 Réau, p. 27., English translation by Douglas Ellis, Department of Linguistics, McGill University, Montreal, PQ. For an analysis of Benedict's encyclical and theology as well as the controversy surrounding representations of the Holy Spirit as a young boy, see François Bœspflug, *Dieu dans l'art*, Cerf, Paris, 1984.

122 DTC, p. 785.     123 DS, p. 1516.

124  Leonid Ouspensky and Vladimir Lossky, *The Meaning of Icons*, St. Vladimir's, Crestwood, 1982, pp. 47-8.

125  *Ibid.*, note 2, pp. 47-8.

126  Dionysius, p. 39, also see notes 1 and 3 for p. 39 in back p. 102.

127  *Ibid.*, p. 42, also see note 10 for p. 42 in back p. 103.

128  *Ibid.*, p. 45, also see note 2 for p. 45 in back p. 104.

129  *Ibid.*, p. 46 also see note 1 given for p. 46 in back p. 104.

130  *Ibid.*, p. 49 also see notes 6 and 9 for p. 49 in back p. 105.

131  Georges Drobot, *Icône de la Nativity [The Christmas Icon]*, *Spiritualité orientale* #15, Abbaye de Bellefontaine, 1975, pp. 268-69.

132  Dionysius., p. 18.   133 *Ibid.*, p. 88.   134 *Ibid.*, p. 87.

135  André Grabar, *Christian Iconography: A Study of Its Origins*, Princeton University Press, Princeton, 1968, p. 112.

136  Walter Lowrie, *Art in the Early Church*, Norton, New York, 1969, p. 72.

137  Grabar, p. 112.   138  *Ibid.*, p. 112-16.

139  *Evangiles avec Peintures Byzantines du XIe Siècle*, 1 and 2, Re-production des 361 Miniatures du Manuscrit grec 74 de la Bibliothèque Nationale, H. Omont, ed., Berthaud Frères, 1908, pp. 6-7.

140  Adelheid Heimann, "L'Iconographie de la Trinité," *L'Art chrétien*, I, October 1934, p. 140.

141  John Martin, *The Illustration of the Heavenly Ladder of St. John Climacus*, Princeton, 1954, pp. 49-50.

142  S. A. Papadopoulos, "Essai d"interprétation du Thème iconographique de la Paternité dans l'Art Byzantin," *Cahiers Archéologiques*,18, 1968, p. 134.

143  Hans Gerstinger, "Uber Herkunft und Entwicklung der Anthropomorphen Byzantinisch-Slavischen Trinitats-darstellungen des Sogenannten Synthronoi-und Paternitas-(Otéchestow) Typus," *Festschrift W. Sas-Zaloziecky zum 60 Gerburtstag*, Akademische Druck-U. Verlagsanstalt, Graz, 1956, pp. 79 ff.

144  Heimann, p. 40.   145  Réau, pp. 25-6.

146  Emile Mâle, *The Religious Art in France: The Twelfth Century*, Princeton, 1978, pp. 182ff.

147  V. Leroquais, *Le Bréviaire de Philippe le Bon*, Bussels, 1927, p. 121, cited from Heimann, note 33, p. 55.

148  Gerstinger, pp. 79 ff.

149  *Ibid.*          150  Heimann, p. 41.

151  Papadopoulos, p. 134.          152  Heimann, p. 41.

153  Ernst Kantorowicz, "The Quinity of Winchester," *The Art Bulletin*, 29.1, March, 1947, pp. 73-85.

154  Jean Lassus, *The Early Christian and Byzantine World*, illustration 84, Hamlyn, London, 1967.

155  Konstantin Kalokyris, *The Byzantine Wall-Paintings of Crete*, Red Dust, New York, 1973, pp. 113-14.

156  Kantorowicz, notes 23 and 24, pp. 76-77.

157  Papadopoulos, note 79, p. 136.

# Canons on Iconography

The following documents are a collection of historical texts dealing with figurative art, iconography. They are canonical in nature, that is, they have been issued by the Church, a council, a particular Church, or a church authority with the intention of regulating the conduct of Christians and artists in relation to figurative art. I do not claim that every historical document has been included; those that are missing, or are incomplete, for whatever reason, can be added later. The purpose is to collect in one volume as many historical texts as possible so that researchers can more easily carry on their work.

## 1. The Church-Orders, Didascalia, Constitutions, and Canons of the Third Century

There is a category of ancient documents dating from the third century to perhaps the beginning of the fourth century, containing canons, prayers, liturgies, moral precepts, etc. They are called Church-orders, or didascalia, and reveal something of the Christians' attitude toward art. It is difficult to date many of the documents because they include various writings of different periods. The fact that they exist in several translations also complicates the problem of dating. After much study and comparison, specialists have come to the conclusion that the didascalia reflect the historical context of the third century during a time of peace, either before or after the persecution of Decius, 248–251.[1]

## A. The Apostolic Tradition of Hippolytus of Rome (AT)

This document was probably written by Hippolytus himself around 215 and contains a very important picture of the life of the Roman Church at the beginning of the third century. It has in one way or another influenced all the didascalia that followed. In its second part, "Of the Laity," we have a list of prohibited crafts and professions; those people who made a living in these areas could not become catechumens without a change of profession.

> On the crafts and professions forbidden to Christians.
>
> If a man be a sculptor or a painter, he shall be taught *not to make idols*. If he will not desist, let him be rejected.[2]

## B. The Didascalia of the Twelve Apostles (DTA)

This document exists only in a Syriac translation; the original Greek text has been lost. It is supposed that the DTA was written in Syria.

> That it is not right to receive gifts of alms from reprehensible persons.
>
> Do you the bishops and the deacons be constant therefore in the ministry of the altar of Christ – we mean the widows and the orphans . . . But if there be bishops who are careless and give no heed to these matters . . . to administer for the nourishment of orphans and widows . . . from *painters of pictures or from makers of idols* . . . they . . . shall be found guilty in judgement in the day of the Lord . . . .[3]

## C. The Ethiopic Didascalia (ED)

This document is another in the same family of didascalia. It generally reproduces the DTA with some variants.

> That the bishop ought to show understanding in receiving offerings from those (only) that are worthy.

The bishop ought to show understanding and make a difference about receiving offerings in cases when it befitteth not . . . Let us keep far from. . . . *them that make idols.*[4]

## D. *The Octateuch of Clement,* the Syriac version (OC)

This constitution in eight books, piously attributed to St. Clement of Rome, is one among several anonymous collections written in various ancient languages.

Ordinance that contains the rule . . . about the order of those to be baptized.

A person *who makes and paints idols* . . . : these are not to be admitted.[5]

Ecclesiastical Canons about those who have recently come to the mystery [of baptism].

I too, Paul, the least of the apostles, give you this command, to you the bishops and priests, about the canons: 6. *The idol maker* who comes forward will stop [making idols] or will be rejected.[6]

## E. *The Egyptian Didascalia (ED)*

If there is *a maker of images or a painter* (zographos), let them be instructed *not to make an idol* (eidolon); either let them leave off or let them be rejected.[7]

## F. *The Arabic Didascalia (AD)*

And if anyone is a *maker of idols or a painter,* let him be taught not to make idols, and if he be not willing to desist, let him be sent away.[8]

## G. *The Canons of Hippolytus ,* Canon 11 (CH)

About anyone who *makes idols and images*, whether maker or painter.

Every artist, let him learn *not to make any image or any idol whatsoever,* whether he be a maker, silversmith, painter, or a worker in any other kind of art. If it happens that, after baptism, any artist makes any such thing, except what people need, let him be cut off until he repents.[9]

Depending on the context of the different ordinances, we have two general kinds of artists: 1) those already in the Church (ED and CH) and 2) those desiring to enter the

Church (AT and OC). The DTA, the AD, and the DE are ambiguous about whether the artists are in the Church already or not. Whatever their relation to the Church, artists who make idols are excluded from her communion.

## 2. Canon 36 of the Council of Elvira, around 300

*Placuit picturas in ecclesia esse non debere, ne quod colitur et adoratur in parietibus depingatur.*[10]

It has seemed good that images should not be in churches so that what is venerated and worshiped not be painted on the walls.

The Council of Elvira in Granada, (present day Spain) met in a period of relative peace, between 295–302 or 306–314. Between these two periods, 302–306, the persecution of Diocletian wrought havoc in the Church. The bishops at Elvira issued 81 canons among which we find the famous canon 36. Because it deals with images in Christian churches, this canon has become the center of great controversy. The problem, of course, is to know how to interpret it; what did it mean to those who issued it? It is not surprising, therefore, that those Christians with an iconophobic tendency see in this canon a confirmation of their point of view. Iconodules, on the other hand, are somewhat embarrassed by an open interdiction of images in churches and try to limit the canon's importance, scope, and meaning.

We have in the Council of Elvira one of the first Christian texts of the pre-Constantinian period that shows that the Christians could distinguish between idols and other images. They could distinguish them not only in theory but also in practice since it is obvious that there would be no images of pagan gods in churches. In the canon, the word *picturas* (images) clearly means non-idolatrous, figurative representations of a Christian character.

This canon is also evidence that the painting of Christian images was not something new at the beginning of the 4th century. It is a bit difficult to imagine that one day around 300, certain Spanish Christians conceived the completely original idea of painting Christian images on the walls of their churches, as though no one had ever heard of such a practice before. The year 300 is too late a date for a simple recognition of the existence of images in a Christian setting: around 200, the Good Shepherd depicted on a chalice in a catholic church in Africa (Tertullian, *On Modesty*, ch. X); between 240 and 256, the wall-paintings of Dura-Europos are executed [11]; and from at least 250, the catacomb paintings appear. In general, ecclesiastical canons, like civil law, especially in the form of prohibitions, are a response to an already existing situation. We can therefore suppose that in Spain at the beginning of the 4th century there already existed churches with painted walls, but for how long we cannot say.

First of all, we are in the dark as to the subjects of the paintings. According to the canon, the subject was, at least in part, "what is venerated and worshiped." If we take the words *colitur* and *adoratur* as synonyms, we should conclude that God the Father, Christ, the Holy Spirit, or all three appeared in the wall-paintings, either in symbols or in "portraits." The meaning of "what is venerated and worshiped" is only one of the problems related to this canon. What the bishops actually prohibited is also a problem: were all sorts of subjects forbidden or just a limited category of images? If we knew the answer to this question, it would be much easier to interpret the canon.

Secondly, we do not know what motivated the bishops to issue the canon. What were the conditions in Spain at that time? Were the bishops afraid of profanation by the pagans, during a period of persecution; were they afraid of superstition among Christians? Without knowing the context in which the bishops conceived their decision, we are left without the tools necessary for arriving at a deeper understanding of the canon.

Thirdly, the reference to the walls, *in parietibus* , adds another factor of ambiguity. Let us suppose that the bishops forbad images of X in churches for reasons Y. It seems that the interdiction applies only to the walls of churches. Are we to assume that these same images were permitted in other places, such as in homes, catacombs, private chapels, on sarcophagi, as for example the Saragossa[12] sarcophagus? The fact that the bishops mentioned the walls specifically is certainly a restriction of the interdiction.

In his book *Power and Sexuality* [13], Laeuchli analyzed the 81 canons from the linguistic point of view and concluded that the very structure of canon 36 – only three other canons have a similar form – indicates that the bishops clearly felt ambivalent about prohibiting images in churches. He established a linguistic structure, applicable to all the canons, made up of five elements: 1) the persons condemned; 2) the cause, what the persons did; 3) the justification of the canon, often in very emotional sentences that highlight the rectitude of the decision; 4) the authority, in general indicated by the word *placuit* , "It has seemed good [to the bishops]" ; 5) the decision itself. In the case of canon 36, there is only an authority (4), *placuit* ; a decision (5), not to do something; and a justification (3). Sections (1) and (2), the persons and the cause, are absent. The absence of an anathema against those who do not conform to the canon adds to what Laeuchli calls the bishops' ambiguity about the question of images; they are not sure whether they should accept or ban them.

Canon 36 has its place in a list of 80 other disciplinary, not theological, canons. Should we, therefore, identify the motive behind it as merely disciplinary, without any theological base? Those of an iconophobic bent tend to see behind the canon an iconophobic theology based on the 2nd commandment, while iconodules are inclined to restrict the canon's scope to the realm of discipline. Two factors nonetheless seem to tip the scales in favor of a limited, disciplinary motive: 1) positively, the canon is part of a series of disciplinary canons, and 2) negatively, we have no indications that the bishops wanted to condemn all kinds of images on the basis of the 2nd commandment or anything else. If canon 36 is, in fact, a disciplinary canon attempting to regulate but not condemn a well-established practice, then the Council of Elvira does not deal with the basic theological question: the legitimacy of Christian images. Another 400 years will have to go by before that question is clearly and directly ask and answered.

We must recognize, however, that for whatever reasons – reasons that we will never really know – it seemed good to a group of bishops in Spain around the year 300 to prohibit the painting of certain *picturas* on church walls. It is fairly obvious that this decision, and the reasons that motivated it, did not affect the Spanish Christians of subsequent history because they continued to paint images on the walls of Spanish churches. As far as we know, there has never been an iconoclastic controversy in the Spanish Church. Canon 36 itself had no subsequent history either, except in the collections of the council's canons preserved here and there. We also know that canon 36 was completely ignored in all other Churches until the Reformation of the 16th century. Even during the Byzantine iconoclastic crisis, the iconoclasts did not quote it in their argumentation. It is quite possible that they did not know about it since few iconoclasts spoke Latin or had many contacts with the West. Due to the great geographic distance between Spain and Byzantium as well as the language barrier, it is not surprising that the iconoclasts never heard about canon 36 of the Council of Elvira.

On the other hand, we cannot really say that the canon was hidden or lost. Several councils of the 4th century adopted certain of Elvira's canons verbatim, but not canon 36. Various canonical collections, however, reproduced it[14]; the iconodules did not, therefore, try to hide it. The canon slept peacefully in these collections, having no great importance, like many other ancient canons that have lost their importance due to a change in the historical setting that gave them birth. It really only came onto the stage of history at the Protestant Reformation. Even though it had existed since the beginning of the 4th century, the canon had no historical importance until the 16th century. Since that time, iconoclasts and iconophobes have used it as a weapon against iconodules both Catholic and Orthodox.

The scope of canon 36 remains very limited in time and space, and very few Protestants of an iconophobic outlook would feel themselves bound by the decision of the synod of Elvira, if we understand that decision as an absolute interdiction of all images on church walls. Only the most radical reformers of the 16th century, and their successors, would advocate a total ban.

To conclude then, we can say that the Council of Elvira really did forbid *picturas* to be painted on the wall of some Spanish churches, but for reasons that we will probably never know. This interdiction, however, is evidence for a tradition of wall-paintings in Spanish churches, going back we do not know how long. The vast majority of Christians, however, both iconoclasts and iconodules, have not given this council, or its canon 36, very much importance or authority. Nor have these Christians felt themselves bound to banish all *picturas* from the walls of their churches. As for the attitude of Spanish Christians toward non-idolatrous images at the beginning of the 4th century, canon 36 is so embroiled in ambiguity that it is practically impossible to arrive at any clear and definitive conclusions. That it is an expression of a generalized iconophobia in the Spanish Church, a repudiation of all figurative art, and a blueprint for an imageless Christianity seems to be a very heavy load indeed to put on the back of such a frail, little donkey.

## 3. The Council of Dvin, Armenia, 554

This council dealt with certain iconoclasts pursued by the Catholicos of the Albanians (the Abkhazians and Aghouans). See the Encyclical of the Catholicos and the *Oath of Union*. Since these documents are in classical Armenian, I have not been able to get translations of them.[15]

## 4. The Quinisext Council, 692

### Canon 73

Since the life-giving cross has shewn to us Salvation, we should be careful that we render due honour to that by which we were saved from the ancient fall. Wherefore, in mind, in word, in feeling giving veneration to it, we command that the figure of the cross, which some have placed on the floor, be entirely removed therefrom, lest the trophy of the victory won for us be desecrated by the trampling under foot of those who walk over it. Therefore those who from this present represent on the pavement the sign of the cross, we decree are to be cut off.[16]

## Canon 82

In some pictures of the venerable icons, a lamb is painted to which the Precursor points his finger, which is received as a type of grace, indicating beforehand through the Law, our true Lamb, Christ our God. Embracing therefore the ancient types and shadows as symbols of the truth, and patterns given to the Church, we prefer 'grace and truth,' receiving it as the fulfillment of the Law. In order therefore that 'that which is perfect' may be delineated to the eyes of all, at least in coloured expression, we decree that the figure in human form of the Lamb who taketh away the sin of the world, Christ our God, be henceforth exhibited in images, instead of the ancient lamb, so that all may understand by means of it the depths of the humiliation of the Word of God, and that we may recall to our memory his conversation in the flesh, his passion and salutary death, and his redemption which was wrought for the whole world.[17]

## Canon 100

'Let thine eyes behold the thing which is right,' orders Wisdom, 'and keep thine heart with all care.' For the bodily senses easily bring their own impressions into the soul. Therefore we order that henceforth there shall in no way be made pictures, whether they are in paintings or in what way so ever, which attract the eye and corrupt the mind, and incite it to the enkindling of base pleasures. And if any one shall attempt to do this he is to be cut off.[18]

# 5. The Council of Rome, Pope St. Gregory II, 727

Hefele:

This council was referred to in a letter of Pope Hadrian I to Charlemagne; Pope Gregory II, and supposedly the council, 'gave an address on the permissibility of the veneration of images' producing 'several of the arguments used, e. g., in regard to the ark of the covenant, the cherubim, to Bezaleel and Aholiab . . . .'[19]

## 6. The Council of Rome, Pope Gregory III, 731

If anyone, for the future, shall take away, destroy, dishonour, or revile the pictures of the Lord or of His Mother, he shall be excluded from the body and blood of the Lord and the communion of the Church.[20]

## 7. The Iconoclastic Council of Hieria, 754

The first seven statements summarize the trinitarian and christological doctrine of the Church as formulated at the 5th and 6th ecumenical councils.

8.    If anyone endeavors to contemplate the divine form of God the Logos in his incarnation through the medium of material colors, and does not worship him with the whole heart, with the eyes of the mind, as he sits *in excelsis* , more dazzling than the sun, at the right hand of God, on the throne of glory, anathema.

9.    If anyone seeks to circumscribe by material colors in images of human form the uncircumscribable substance and hypostasis of God the Logos because of the incarnation, and does not, on the contrary, teach that he is nonetheless uncircumscribable even after the incarnation, anathema.

10. If anyone attempts to portray in an image the inseparable hypostatic union of the nature of the God the Logos and his flesh, or the One Person, unconfused and undivided, that arose out of the two natures, calling it Christ – since the name Christ signifies both God and man – and thus monstrously contriving a confusion of the two natures, anathema.

11. If anyone isolates the flesh united to the hypostasis of God the Logos, considering it by itself in mere thought, and hence sets out to make an image of it, anathema.

12. If anyone divides the One Christ into two hypostases, separating the son of God from the son of the Virgin Mary, and does not confess him to be one and the same, but argues that the union of the two is a relative one, so that he may

119

portray the son of the Virgin as if he had a separate hypostasis, anathema.

13. If anyone represents in an image the flesh divinized by union with the divine Logos, as if separating it from the Godhead, which assumed it and deified it, and therefore picturing it as devoid of divinity, anathema.

14. If anyone tries to depict in lifeless colors God the Logos, who, existing in the form of God, assumed the form of a servant in his own hypostasis and became in all respects like us, except for sin regarding him as if he were a mere man, and seeks to separate him from his inseparable and unchangeable divinity, thus introducing a fourth member into the holy and life-giving Trinity, anathema.

15. If anyone does not acknowledge Mary, ever a virgin, to be properly and truly Mother of God, and higher than all creation, visible and invisible, and does not with sincere faith entreat intercession of her, as one who has the privilege of speaking openly to our God, whom she bore, anathema.

16. If anyone ventures to set up profitless figures of all the saints in lifeless, speechless images made of material colors – for this is a vain invention and the discovery of diabolical craft – and does not, on the contrary, reproduce their virtues in himself as animate, living images with the aid of what has been revealed about them in books, in order to be stimulated to zeal similar to theirs, as our inspired fathers have said, anathema.

17. If anyone does not confess that all the saints from the beginning of time until the present day, who pleased God before the law, under the law, and under grace, are honored in his sight both in soul and body, and does not, according to the tradition of the Church, entreat their prayers since they have the boldness to intercede for the world, anathema.

18. If anyone does not confess the resurrection of the dead, the judgment, and the reward to each according to his deserts by the righteous scales of God, and does not confess that there is no end of punishment or of the heavenly kingdom, which is the enjoyment of God, 'for the kingdom of

heaven,' according to the divine apostle (Rm 14:17) 'is not meat and drink, but righteousness, and peace, and joy in the Holy Spirit,' anathema.

19. If anyone does not accept this, our holy seventh ecumenical council, but criticizes it in any way, and does not endorse without reserve what it has decreed in accordance with the teaching of divinely inspired Scripture, anathema from the Father, and the Son, and the Holy Spirit, and the seven ecumenical councils.

20. These things having been determined by us with all precision and unity, we ordain that no one shall be permitted to set forth any doctrine other than this or to write, or contrive, or think, or teach contrary to it; and that any who dare to devise, or bring forward, or teach, or impart a different doctrine to those who wish to be converted from any heresy whatsoever to the acknowledgment of the truth, or [who dare] to introduce novelty of expression or innovation of language in order to overturn these, our decrees, shall, if bishops or clergy, be deposed, the bishops from their bishopric, the clergy from orders, and shall, if monks or laymen, be anathematized."[21]

## 8. The Council of Gentilly, 767

Hefele:

The acts of this council, convoked by Pepin, king of the Franks, to examine the question of images have been lost. The iconoclastic ambassadors from Constantinople hoped to obtain Pepin's condemnation of images. Since Pope Paul I seemed to be satisfied with the results of this council, we can assume that Pepin and his council reaffirmed the legitimacy of the veneration of images.[22]

## 9. The Council of the Lateran, Pope Stephen III, 769

Hefele:

The fourth session was occupied with the question of the veneration of images. Patristic testimonies for this were presented, the Council of Constantinople of the year 754 was anathematized, and that veneration recognized for the images which had been shown to them until this time by all Popes and reverend Fathers. In this session, too, that Synodica of the Patriarch Theodore of Jerusalem . . . was read and approved. At the same time, Pope Stephen appealed to the picture of Agbarus [Abgar] . . . since by that Christ Himself had confirmed the veneration of images.[23]

## 10. The Seventh Ecumenical Council (Nicaea II), 787

The holy, great, and Ecumenical Council . . . having followed the tradition of the catholic Church, has defined the following:

Christ our God, Who granted to us the light of His knowledge and Who delivered us from the darkness of the insanity of the idols . . . commanded that she [the Church] may be so preserved. He also gave assurances to his holy disciples, saying: 'I am with you always, to the close of the age.' (Mt 28:20) He gave this commandment not only to his disciples but also to us who through them have believed in his name.

However, some men, paying no regard to this gift, and encouraged by the deceitful enemy, deviated from right thinking and, after opposing the tradition of the catholic Church, erred in the perception of truth . . . . For, having followed men of impiety who put faith in their own minds, they have accused the holy Church, which has been joined to Christ the God, and they have made no distinction between the holy and the profane, calling the icon of the Lord and those of his saints with the same name as the wooden symbols of the idols of Satan.

For this reason God the sovereign One, not bearing to see his people destroyed by such a pestilence, through his good will brought us, the leaders of the priesthood, together from all parts . . . so that the divine tradition of the catholic Church may regain its authority by a common vote. Having, therefore, sought most diligently and conferred with each other, and having set as our goal the truth, we neither delete nor add anything, but preserve undiminished everything that is of the catholic Church. Adhering also to the six holy Ecumenical Councils . . . .

In summary, we preserve all the traditions of the Church, which for our sake have been decreed in written or unwritten form, without introducing an innovation. One of these traditions is the making of iconographic representations – being in accordance with the narrative of the proclamation of the gospel – for the purpose of ascertaining the incarnation of God the Word, which was real, not imaginary, and for being of an equal benefit to us as the gospel narrative. For those which point mutually to each other undoubtedly mutually signify each other.

Be this as it may, and continuing along the royal pathway, following both the teaching of our holy Fathers which is inspired by God and the tradition of the catholic Church – for we know that this tradition is of the holy Spirit dwelling in her – in absolute precision and harmony with the spirit, we declare that, next to the sign of the precious and life-giving cross, venerable and holy icons – made of colours, pebbles, or any other material that is fit – may be set in the holy churches of God, on holy utensils and vestments, on walls and boards, in houses and in streets. These may be icons of our Lord and God the Saviour Jesus Christ, or of our pure Lady the holy Theotokos, or of honourable angels, or of any saint or holy man.

For the more these are kept in view through their iconographic representations, the more those who look at them are lifted up to remember and have an earnest desire for the prototypes. Also [we declare] that one may render to them the veneration of honour: not the true worship of our faith, which is due only to the divine nature, but the same kind of veneration as is offered to the form of the precious and life-giving cross, to the holy gospels, and to the other holy dedicated items. Also [we declare] that one may honour these by bringing to them incense and light, as was the pious custom of the early [Christians]; for 'the honour to the icon is conveyed to the prototype.' [Basil of Caesarea, *On the Holy Spirit*] Thus, he who venerates the icon venerates the hypostasis of the person depicted on it. In this way the teaching of our holy Fathers – that is, the tradition of the catholic Church, which has accepted the gospel from one end of the earth to the other – is strengthened. Thus, we faithfully follow Paul, who spoke in Christ, as well as the entire divine assembly of the Apostles and holy Fathers, 'holding the traditions which we have received.' [2 Th 2:15 and 3:6]

Hence those who take the liberty of thinking or teaching otherwise, or – like the accursed heretics – of violating the traditions of the Church and inventing some sort of novelty, or of rejecting some of the things which have been dedicated to the Church – that is the gospel, or the form of the cross, or an iconographic representation, or a holy relic of a martyr – or of contriving crookedly and cunningly to upset any of the legitimate traditions of the catholic Church, or of using the holy treasures or the venerable monasteries as a common place, if they are bishops or clergymen, we direct that they be unfrocked; if monks or laymen of the society, that they be excommunicated."[24]

## 11. The Council of Frankfurt, 794

### Canon 2

We have examined the decision of the Greek council held in Constantinople [Nicaea II] which anathematizes anyone who will not give to images of the saints *servitium* and *adoratio* as these are given to the Trinity. All the bishops present refused to give *adoratio* and *servitium* to images; they also rejected this council unanimously."[25]

The preceding text is canon 2 of the Council of Frankfurt. The following text, mistakenly attributed by Ouspensky to the Council of Frankfurt, is in reality a passage from the *Libri Carolini*, Charlemagne's theological treatise against Nicaea II.[26]

Neither one nor the other deserves the title of 'seventh.' Believing in the Orthodox doctrine which states that images should only be used to decorate churches, and in memory of past canons according to which we should adore only God and venerate the saints, we do not want to prohibit images as does one of these councils or to adore them as does the other, and we reject the writings of this ridiculous council."[27]

## 12. The Iconoclastic Council of Hagia Sophia, 815

This Council [the Council of Hieria, 754], having confirmed and fortified the divine doctrines of the holy Fathers and followed [the lead of] the six holy Ecumenical Councils, formulated [a set of] most pious canons; wherefore the Church of God remained untroubled for many years and guarded the people in peace; until it chanced that the imperial office passed from [the hands of] men into [those of] a woman, and God's Church was undone by female frivolity: for, guided by most ignorant bishops, she convened a thoughtless assembly [the 7th Ecumenical Council] and put forward the doctrine that the incomprehensible Son and Logos of God should be painted [as He was] during the Incarnation by means of dishonored matter. She also heedlessly stated that lifeless portraits of the most-holy Mother of God and the saints who shared in His [Christ's] form should be set up and worshipped, thereby coming into conflict with the central doctrine of the Church. Further she confounded our worship by arbitrarily affirming that what is fit for God should be offered to the inanimate matter of icons, and she senselessly dared state that these were filled with divine grace, and by offering them candlelight and sweet-smelling incense as well as forced veneration, she led the simpleminded into error . . . . Wherefore, taking to heart the correct doctrine, we banish from the Catholic Church the unwarranted manufacture of the spurious icons that has been so audaciously proclaimed, impelled as we are by a judicious judgment; nay, by passing a righteous judgment upon the veneration of icons that has been injudiciously proclaimed by Tarasius [the patriarch at the time of the 7th Ecumenical Council], and so refuting it, we declare his assembly invalid in that it bestowed exaggerated honor to painting, namely, as has already been said, the lighting of candles and lamps and the offering of incense, these marks of veneration being those of worship. We gladly accept, on the other hand, the pious council [the Council of Hieria, 754] that was held at Blachernae, in the church of the All-Pure Virgin, under the former pious Emperors Constantine and Leo, a council that was fortified by the doctrine of the Fathers, and in preserving without alteration what was expressed by it, we decree that the manufacture of icons is unfit for veneration and useless. We refrain, however, from calling them idols since there is a distinction between different kinds of evil.[28]

## 13. The Council of Paris, 825

In a letter written to the emperor, Louis the Pious, and to his son Lothar, the Frankish bishops criticized certain parts of the letter Pope Hadrian I sent to the empress Irene and her son, at the time of Nicaea II in 787.

He [Pope Hadrian I] had asked that images be exposed, worshiped, and called holy; however, if the exposition of images is permitted, the worship of them is not. Hadrian had quoted the testimony of the Fathers, but his choice was not good for the texts were *valde absona et ad rem de qua agebatur minime pertinentia*. A council was then held in the East [Nicaea II, 787], but as the first one, held under Constantine Copronymus [the Council of Hieria, 754], erred by forbidding images, this new council fell into an error no less serious by ordering the worship of images, giving them the title of holy, and attributing to them the privilege of holiness. Charlemagne had already sent the priest Angilbert to Rome, carrying a text against this council. [The *Libri Carolini* ?] In his answer, the pope [Hadrian I] defended the proofs brought forward by this council and wrote *quae voluit, non tamen quae decuit*. Thus, without in any way attacking the authority of the pope, it is possible to believe that his answer contained several things contrary to the truth. At the end of his defense, the pope [Hadrian I] claimed to teach the doctrine of Gregory the Great on this matter. He therefore did not go astray by ignorance.

The Frankish bishops [at the Council of Paris] said that they then had read the letter given to the emperor [Louis] the preceding year by the Greek ambassadors. Freculf and Adegar made known their proceedings in Rome [to Pope Eugene II]. It is well known that the emperors [Louis and Lothar] had taken the middle road between the extremists, both iconoclast and iconodule. They had wanted to cure these two equally sick factions, but the error was defended in places where it should have been condemned (in Rome). God then indicated to the emperors another path to take by inspiring them to ask the pope's [Eugene's] permission to undertake an inquiry of this question, whose results they would publish, so that every authority would be required, whether they wanted to or not, to bow before the truth. Prudence required, moreover, that, in the declarations sent by the emperor [Louis], all reprimands should be inserted against both the friends and enemies of images. This should especially be done in the letter to the Greeks, but in a moderate and respectful tone, especially in reference to Rome, while still making known the whole truth. The pope [Eugene] then issued only one ordinance in line with the real state of affairs, out of respect for the emperors, for the authority of his see, and for the evidence brought forward in favor of the truth. The emperors were asked to choose what seemed to them the most appropriate of the passages in the Bible and the Fathers, passages the bishops had put together, and that they [the bishops] sent to them [Louis and Lothar] by Halitgar of Cambrai and Amalaire de Metz. They [the bishops] had had too little time to make this choice themselves, all the more so because all those who had been ordered to appear in the assembly did not show up, for example Moduin, bishop of Autun, who could not come because he was sick.

Canons 1–2 were directed against the iconoclasts.

Canons 3–16 were directed against the iconodules: the veneration of images was said to go back to Simon Magus and Epicures; *latria* is only to be given to God; what comes from the hand of man should be neither venerated nor worshiped; it is unjust to compare the holy Cross and images . . .[29]

## 14. The First–Second Council of Constantinople, 861

This council opposed iconoclasm, but its acts have been lost.[30]

## 15. The Council of Constantinople (the 8th Ecumenical Council for Roman Catholics), 869–870

### Canon 3

We ordain that the holy icon of our Lord be venerated in the same way as the book of the Gospels. Indeed, just as all receive salvation through the syllables contained in it, so do all, both learned and ignorant, draw profit from what the colors of the icon possess. For that which words announce through syllables, the colors in painting show. If one does not venerate the icons of Christ the Savior, let him not see His face at the Second Coming. In the same manner, we venerate and bring homage to the icon of His All-Pure Mother, to those of the holy angels, painted as they are described in the words of Holy Scripture, and furthermore to those of all the saints. Let those who do not do this be anathema.[31]

### Canon 7

To make holy and precious icons, as well as to teach one's neighbors the precepts of divine and human wisdom, is very useful, and not to be done by the unworthy. The excommunicated are therefore not allowed to paint icons in the holy churches nor, by the same token, teach there unless they abjure their errors. If someone, after we have made this decision, starts painting holy icons in churches, he will be deposed if he is a cleric, and deprived of the divine Mysteries if he is a layman.[32]

## 16. The Russian Council Against the Judaizers, Moscow, October 1490

Many of you have mocked the images of Christ and of the All-Pure represented on the icons, while others mocked the Cross of Christ. Still others have uttered words of blasphemy against the holy icons. Others, finally, have destroyed holy icons with axes and burned them in the fire . . . Others among them have thrown icons away. You have reviled the holy image of those who are painted on the icons."[33]

# 17. The Diocesan Council of Sens, France, 1528

This council in Paris recalled that images are acceptable as ways of reminding the faithful of past events and of supporting and sustaining the people's piety.[34]

# 18. The Council of the Hundred Chapters (Stoglav), Moscow, 1551

Chapter 5, question 3: On the holy and venerable icons

The holy and venerable icons, following the divine rules, must reproduce the image of God, his likeness, and be faithful to the established model. Artists will paint the images of God, of the most pure Mother of God, and of all the holy intercessors [according to these rules]. On this matter, you have a statement in the holy Scriptures.

You must pay great attention to icon-painters making sure that they have irreproachable feelings, practice virtue, and instruct their apprentices to learn to paint divine images with skill and according to the established model."[35]

Chapter 27: On the holy icons and the necessity of correcting the books

The archpriests, the dean-priests, the priests assigned to this task, all priests, in each city, in all the holy churches, will inspect the holy icons, sacred vessels . . . .

If any icons have been damaged or have deteriorated over time, they [the clergy] will have them repaired by painters: those icons that are not sufficiently coated with oil will be covered with oil.[36]

Chapter 41, question 1: On the icons of the Trinity

On the icons of the Holy Trinity, some represent a cross in the nimbus of only the middle figure, others on all three. On ancient and on Greek icons, the words 'Holy Trinity' are written at the top, but there is no cross in the nimbus of any of the three. At present, 'IC XC' and 'the Holy Trinity' are written next to the central figure. Consult the divine canons and tell us which practice one should follow.

The Reply: painters must paint icons according to the ancient models, as the Greeks painted them, as Andrei Rublev and other renowned painters made them. The inscription should be: 'the Holy Trinity.' Painters are in no way to use their imagination."[37]

Chapter 41, question 7: On the icons this inscription is written: 'Come, O Peoples, let us adore the Divinity in three Persons.'

It is written on some icons, 'Come, O Peoples, let us adore the Divinity in three Persons.' There, at the bottom, tsars, princes, prelates, and people of lower standing are represented while they were still alive. We must reflect on this matter.

Another example: They are painted even on the icon of the All-Pure Mother of God in Tikhvin, which describes her miracles. We must reflect on this remembering the writings of the holy Fathers. Is it proper on icons to include both the living and the dead at prayer?"[38]

[The italicized passages in the following text come from Ouspensky.]

Answer: The ancient traditions of the holy Fathers, well-known icon-painters, both Greeks and Russians, bear witness [to the fact that it is proper to paint the living and dead]; the holy icons, as well, represent and show such persons. The icon of the Exaltation of the venerable and life-giving Cross represents tsars, prelates, princes, and men of every condition, in great numbers. The icon of the Intercession of the All-Pure Mother of God, which commemorates the day when St. Andrew saw her praying for the world in company of all the saints, represents a great number of people. On the icon that recalls the origin of the venerable Cross, not only tsars and princes but also a great number of people are painted. On the icons of the Last Judgment, there are *not only saints painted but also a great number of unbelievers from various countries.*[39]

Chapter 43: Answer of the assembly on the icon-painters and on the venerable icons.

Following the orders of the tsar, in the sovereign city of Moscow, in all the cities, the metropolitan, the archbishops, the bishops, will pay great attention to the way the liturgy is performed and especially to the holy icons and icon-painters.

They [the prelates] will make sure that all is done according to the sacred rules. They will determine the obligations of the icon-painters, will say according to what rules they [the painters] must paint the bodily representation of God our Lord, of Jesus Christ our Savior, of his most chaste Mother, of the heavenly powers, and of all the saints who, from all time, have been pleasing to God.

The painter must be filled with humility, gentleness, and piety: he will flee from frivolous speech and joking. His character will be peaceful, and he will know nothing of envy. He will not drink, pillage, or steal. Above all, he will observe, with scrupulous attention, spiritual and bodily purity. If he cannot live in chastity till the end [of his life], he will marry according to the law and take a wife. He will frequently visit his spiritual fathers, inform them of all his behavior, fast, pray according to their instructions and lessons, have pure and chaste habits, and know nothing of impudence and disorder.

He will paint the image of our Lord Jesus Christ, of his very chaste Mother, etc., with scrupulous care, according to the likeness, according to the established model, with his eyes fixed on the works of previous painters. He will take the best icons as models. If these painters, our contemporaries, live faithfully according to the instructions that have been given to them, if they accomplish with care this work which is most pleasing to God, they will be rewarded by the tsar; the prelates will watch over them and pay them greater respect than to ordinary people.

These painters will take apprentices, watch over them, teach them piety and purity, and take them to their spiritual fathers who will teach them, according to the rules they have received from their bishops, what kind of life is proper for a Christian: one that is exempt of impudence and disorder.

Let the apprentices follow carefully the lessons of their masters. If an apprentice, by the grace of God, shows great artistic talent, the master will take him to the bishop who will examine the icon painted by the apprentice to see if it reproduces the true image and likeness and will carry out a thorough inquiry about the apprentice to see if he is leading a pure and pious life according to the rules, a life free of all disorder. The bishop will then bless him and invite him to live from then on in piety and to practice his holy profession with undying zeal. The bishop will give him the signs of honor that are given to his master, signs that he does not give to people of low social rank. And finally, the bishop will warn the painter that he must not favor his brother, son, or relatives. If, by the will of God, anyone is without artistic talent or is a mediocre painter, if he does not live according to the regular commitment he has taken on, and if his master declares him competent and an expert, showing the work of another while saying that this apprentice is the author, the bishop, after inquiry, will punish that master according to the prescribed punishments so that other painters, filled with fear, will be dissuaded from following his example. As for the apprentice, he will be absolutely forbidden to paint icons.

If an apprentice, by the will of God, is gifted with certain talents and lives according to the regular commitment that he has taken on, and if his master denounces him out of jealousy, in order to deprive him of the honor he himself enjoys, the bishop, after inquiry, will punish this master according to the prescribed punishments, and the apprentice will receive an even greater honor.

If one of these painters hides the talent that God gave him and refuses to allow his apprentices to benefit from it, he will be condemned by God, to eternal suffering, like the one who buried his talent. If one of these masters or one of their apprentices does not live according to the regular commitment he has taken on, if he gets drunk, lives in impurity and disorder, the bishops will forbid him to paint icons, fearing the sentence of the prophet: 'Cursed is he who does the work of the Lord with slackness . . .' [Jer 48: 10][40]

*Let those who up to now have painted icons without having learned to, who paint fancifully, without either practice or conformity to the image,[41] have their works taken away from them and sold to simple and ignorant people in the villages for next to nothing: the painters of these icons will[42] be obliged to learn from good masters.*

*"Whoever, by the grace of God, starts painting according to the image and likeness, let him paint. Let the one from whom God has withheld such a gift abandon painting alto-*

*gether, so that the name of God may not be blasphemed by such paintings.*[43] If anyone breaks this ruling, let him be punished by the tsar and brought to judgment. If some people answer you this way, 'This trade provides us with a living; it is our daily bread,' do not be swayed by this objection because it is their ignorance that is speaking, and they do not feel guilty of any sin. Everyone cannot paint icons: God has given men various trades and professions, other than icon-painting. These other livelihoods are capable of feeding them and assuring their subsistence. The image of God must not be given to those who disfigure it and dishonor it.[44]

*In all towns and villages and monasteries of their diocese, the archbishops and bishops will inspect the icon-painters and will personally examine their works.*[45] They will choose, each in his own diocese, the best-known painters and give them the right of inspecting their fellow painters so that there will be no clumsy or vulgar painters among them.[46] *The archbishops and bishops will personally assess the painters they have charged with supervising the others, and will control them rigorously.*[47] These supervisors will be given honors and will receive special signs of esteem. The great lords and the humble people will honor these painters and will respect their venerable art.[48]

*The prelates, each in his own diocese, will carefully and with unflagging attention see to it that the good iconographers, and their apprentices, paint according to the ancient models, and do not depict the divinity according to their own concept or assumptions. If Christ our God can be depicted in the flesh, He is not depictable according to His Divinity; as John of Damascus has it, 'Do not represent the divinity. You, blind ones, do not lie because the Godhead is simple and indivisible, inaccessible to the eye. But in representing the image of the flesh, I venerate and believe, and I glorify the Virgin who gave birth to the Son . . .'*[49]

If a painter, having been trained by experienced and expert masters, hides the talent God has given him and does not train his apprentices in his art, let him be condemned by Christ to eternal punishment, like the one who buried his talent. Therefore, painters, instruct your apprentices without any kind of clever restrictions, so as not to be condemned to eternal punishment.[50]

Chapter 74: Answer concerning the holy and venerable icons

We see monks and nuns, poor people, beggar-women, and lay people wandering around the countryside, in the cities, in the streets, on estates, in the districts, and in the villages. They go all over carrying holy icons. Some of these people, troubled by dreams and seduced by demons, pass themselves off as prophets and collect money for the construction of churches; others solicit money to ransom prisoners. They appear in the markets with icons. This spectacle is a scandal. The people of other countries and on-lookers of other religions are surprised to see them wandering around with holy icons.

The Scriptures say, 'Render to divine things the honor that is due to them.' And again they say, 'Cursed is he who does the work of the Lord with slackness . . .' [Jer 48: 10] The tsar must issue a decree on this matter and loudly announce in the markets that it is forbidden for people of this sort to carry holy icons. Those who beg in order to pay a ransom or for other needs will solicit in God's name from religious people, but, under no circumstances, are they to show themselves in public with icons in hand. If anyone goes against this prohibition, his icons are to be taken away from him and deposited in the holy churches. He is to be chased out of the cities so that his punishment will discourage others from engaging in similar practices."[51]

## 19. The Council of Moscow, 1553–1554

A layman named Viskovatyi protested to Metropolitan Macarius against images of God the Father, and other novelties, recently introduced. The metropolitan and the council condemned Viskovatyi and approved images of God the Father on the basis of Old Testament visions. The decision, though it is not a canon, was still important because it showed the mentality of the leaders of the Moscow Church at a moment when two different visions of iconography collided head on.[52]

# 20. The Council of Trent, 1545–49, 1551–52, 1562–63

## Session 25

Touching the Invocation, Veneration, and on Relics of Saints and Sacred Images

The holy synod enjoins on all bishops, and others sustaining the office and charge of teaching, that, according to the usage of the Catholic and Apostolic Church, received from the primitive times of the Christian religion, and according to the consent of the holy fathers, and to the decrees of sacred councils, they especially instruct the faithful diligently touching . . . the lawful use of images . . . .

Moreover, that the images of Christ, of the Virgin Mother of God, and of the other saints, are to be had and retained particularly in temples, and that due honour and veneration are to be awarded them; not that any divinity or virtue is believed to be in them, on account of which they are to be worshipped; or that anything is to be asked of them; or that confidence is to be reposed in images, as was of old done by the Gentiles, who placed their hope in idols; but because the honour which is shown unto them is referred to the prototypes which they represent; in such wise that by the images which we kiss, and before which we uncover the head, and prostrate ourselves, we adore Christ, and venerate the saints, whose similitude they bear. And this, by the decrees of councils, and especially of the second synod of Nicaea, has been ordained against the opponents of images.

And the bishops shall carefully teach this; that, by means of the histories of the mysteries of our Redemption, depicted by paintings or other representations, the people are instructed, and strengthened in remembering, and continually reflecting on the articles of faith; as also that great profit is derived from all sacred images, not only because the people are thereby admonished of the benefits and gifts which have been bestowed upon them by Christ, but also because the miracles of God through the means of the saints, and their salutary examples, are set before the eyes of the faithful; that so for those things they may give God thanks; may order their own life and manners in imitation of the saints; and may be excited to adore and love God, and to cultivate piety. But if any one shall teach or think contrary to these decrees; let him be anathema. And if any abuses have crept in amongst these holy and salutary observances, the holy synod earnestly desires that they be utterly abolished; in such wise that no image conducive to false doctrine, and furnishing occasion of dangerous error to the uneducated, be set up. And if at times, when it shall be expedient for the unlearned people; it happen that the histories and narratives of holy scripture are portrayed and represented; the people shall be taught, that not thereby is the Divinity represented, as though it could be perceived by the eyes of the body, or be depicted by colours or figures. Moreover, in the invocation of saints, the veneration of relics, and the sacred use of images, every superstition shall be removed, all filthy lucre be abolished, finally, all lasciviousness be avoided; in such wise that figures shall not be painted or adorned with a wantonness of beauty; nor shall men also pervert the celebration of the saints, and the visitation of relics, into revellings and drunkenness; as if festivals are celebrated to the honour of the saints by luxury and wantonness . . . .

And that these things may be the more faithfully observed, the holy synod ordains, that it be lawful for no one to place, or cause to be placed, any unusual image in any place, or church, howsoever exempted, except it shall have been approved of by the bishop . . . .[53]

## 21. The Synod of Daimper, India, 1599

When the Portuguese established trading stations in Southwest India in the sixteenth century , they found the Thomas Christians who claimed to have been evangelized by St. Thomas himself. These ancient Christians apparently had no images in their churches. Archbishop Menezes called a synod at Daimper in 1599 to impose the decrees of the Council of Trent on the Thomas Christians. The following measure was adopted to introduce images into the native Christians' churches.

*Session VIII, Decree XXIX*

Whereas almost all the churches of this docese are without pictures, which was the effect of their being governed by Nestorian heretics, who do not allow of the healthful use of sacred images; therefore the Synod doth command, that in churches that are finished, the first work that shall be done after that of the baptismal font out of the alms of the parish, shall be to set up some images, according to the directions of the prelate, who shall always be consulted about every picture; and after that of the high altar is once set up, if the church has any side altars, they shall also have images set up in them, and on every altar besides an image, there shall be a cross or [sic, of] some matter or other set up; and in all churches that are large enough and yet have no pulpits, pulpits shall be erected for the preaching of the word of God . . .[54]

## 22. Pope Urban VIII, August 11, 1628

Condemnation of the three-headed Trinity: " . . . Urban VIII ordered the burning of certain paintings that showed the Most Holy Trinity as a man with three faces."[55]

## 23. The Great Council of Moscow, 1666–1667

Chapter 43: On the Iconographer and the Lord Sabaoth

We decree that a skilled painter, who is also a good man (from the ranks of the clergy) be named monitor of the iconographers, their leader and supervisor. Let the ignorant not mock the ugly and badly painted holy icons of Christ, of His Mother, His saints. Let all vanity of pretended wisdom cease, which has allowed everyone habitually to paint the Lord Sabaoth in various representations according to his own fantasy, without an authentic reference . . . . We decree that from now on the image of the Lord Sabaoth will no longer be painted according to senseless and unsuitable imaginings, for no one has ever seen the Lord Sabaoth (that is, God the Father) in the flesh. Only Christ was seen in the flesh, and in this way He is portrayed, that is, in the flesh and not according to his divinity. Likewise, the most holy Mother of God and other saints of God . . . .

To paint on icons the Lord Sabaoth (that is, the Father) with a white beard holding the only-begotten Son in his lap with a dove between them is altogether absurd and improper, for no one has ever seen the Father in His divinity. Indeed, the Father has no flesh, and it is not in the flesh that the Son was born of the Father before all ages. And if the Prophet David says, 'from the womb, before the morning star, I have begotten you' [Ps 109| 110: 3], such generation is certainly not corporeal, but unutterable and unimaginable. For Christ himself says in the Holy Gospel, 'No one knows the Father except the Son.' In chapter 40, Isaiah asks: 'What likeness will you find for God or what form to resemble his?' Likewise, the holy Apostle Paul says in chapter 17 of Acts: 'Since we are God's offspring, we ought not to believe that the Godhead is the same as gold, silver, or stone shaped by human art and thought.' St. John of Damascus likewise says: 'Who can make an imitation of God the invisible, the incorporeal, the undescribable, and unimaginable? To make an image of the Divinity is the height of folly and impiety' [*On the Heavens* , Bk IV, on the image]. St. Gregory Dialogos forbade it in a similar way. This is why the Lord Sabaoth, who is the Godhead, and the engendering before all ages of the only-begotten Son of the Father must only be perceived through our mind. By no means is it proper to paint such images: it is impossible. And the Holy Spirit is not, in His nature, a dove: He is by nature God. And no one has ever seen God, as the holy evangelist points out. Nonetheless, the Holy Spirit appeared in the form of a dove at the holy baptism of Christ in the Jordan; and this is why it is proper to represent the Holy Spirit in the form of a dove, in this context only. Anywhere else, those who have good sense do not represent the Holy Spirit in the form of a dove, for on Mount Tabor He appeared in the form of a cloud, and in another way elsewhere. Besides, Sabaoth is not the name of the Father only, but of the Holy Trinity. According to Dionysius the Areopagite, Sabaoth is translated from the Hebrew as 'Lord of Host.' And the Lord of Hosts is the Trinity. And if the Prophet Daniel says that he has seen the Ancient of Days sitting on the throne of judgment, that is not taken to mean the Father, but the Son at His Second Coming, who will judge all the nations with His fearsome judgment.

Likewise, on icons of the Holy Annunciation, they paint the Lord Sabaoth breathing from His mouth, and that breath reaches the womb of the Most Holy Mother of God. But who has seen this, or which passage from Holy Scripture bears witness to it? Where is this taken from? Such a practice and others like it are clearly adopted and borrowed from people whose understanding is vain, or rather whose mind is deranged or absent. This is why we decree that henceforth such mistaken painting cease, for it comes from unsound knowledge. It is only in the Apocalypse of St. John that the Father can be painted with white hair, for lack of any other possibility, because of the visions contained in it.

It is good and proper to place a cross, that is, the Crucifixion of our Lord and Savior Jesus Christ, above the Deisis in the holy churches in place of Lord Sabaoth, according to the norm preserved since ancient times in all the holy churches of the eastern countries, in Kiev, and everywhere else except in the Muscovite State. This is a great mystery kept by the holy Church . . . .

We say this to shame the iconographers so that they stop making false and vain paintings, and from now on paint nothing according to their own ideas, without an authentic reference.[56]

## 24. Pope Alexander VIII, December 7, 1690

The pope condemned the following proposition found in the *Catéchisme* of Jean Hassels, 1595: "It is impious to place an image of God the Father, shown in a seated position, in a Christian temple."[57]

## 25. Pope Benedict XIV, Sollicitudini Nostrae, 1745

8.    . . . and our letter would stop there if you had not stated in yours that you wanted to inform us of still other points, among which the most important being the publication and the wide distribution of certain images of the Holy Spirit in the form of a handsome young man . . . . Seeing that these images have multiplied to such a degree and spread practi-

cally everywhere, two matters must be clarified: the first is to know if Sister Crescence is the one who created, popularized, or approved them; the second is to determine if the use, the production, and the veneration of this sort of icon can be permitted inside or outside churches.

10. On the second matter, the first thing to be said is that we praise and approve the apostolic zeal with which you, Brother, have ordered that the images of this kind be removed and taken away . . . .

11.

It is certainly lost on no one what an impious and sacrilegous error it would be, quite unworthy of the divine nature, to imagine that anyone can represent in colors the All-Good and Great God as he is in himself. In fact, no one can paint or represent his image in any way other than by a material image of a physical form with all its bodily parts. If anyone attributed these qualities to the divine nature, he would automatically fall into the error of those who give a human form to God (anthropomorphites).

12. However, God is represented in the manner and in the form by which, as we read in the Holy Scriptures, he has deigned to appear to mortals . . . .

13. . . . Petau shows that it is legitimate to paint God according to the form in which, as we have heard, he himself has become visible: 'With the common agreement of Catholics, the following opinion has over time been accepted: God can assuredly be represented to the degree that he has presented himself to men in a visible manner in whatever exterior features.'

14. The holy Council of Trent in no way condemned images representing God in this manner. . . . Therefore, when anyone . . . dares to criticize the use of this kind of image, he opens himself to an ecclesiastical sentence as we learn from the XVth of the propositions condemned on December 7, 1690, by our predecessor of blessed memory, Pope Alexander VIII. This proposition said that 'it is impious to place an image of God the Father, shown in a seated position, in a Christian temple.'

15. In fact, since we read in the Holy Letters that God himself became visible to men in such and such a form, why is it not permitted to paint him in these same forms?

16. Seeing that these undoubted principles have been set out, we can easily understand how painters must draw the image of the Holy Spirit, what images of him are to be approved and which ones disapproved.

17. As for the question before us now, since the Holy Spirit appeared in former times in the visible form of a dove, it is quite certain that that is the form in which his image should be painted.

21. In addition, we read in the sacred pages of the New Testament that after the Ascension of Christ into heaven, while the apostles and the disciples were gathered together with Mary . . . 'there appeared to them tongues as of fire, distributed and resting on each one of them.' (Acts 2: 3) . . . we have taught that to represent what the Church celebrates on the feast of Pentecost, 'it is permitted for painters to represent the apostles with all those who were present with them at the gathering, as well as the tongues of fire descending from heaven and falling like rain on all their heads.' . . . And in the *Catechism* published by the decree of the holy Council of Trent, about this commandment of the decalogue ('You shall have no other gods before me.') in which the question of the representation of the divine Persons is dealt with, we read the following: 'The forms of the dove and the tongues of fire, in the Gospel and the Acts of the Apostles, symbolize the characteristics of the Holy Spirit. It is quite unnecessary to explain this further since it is so well known.'

22. Since it is not legitimate to show men the image of a divine Person in any other form than the one, according to the Holy Scriptures, in which this Person deigned, in former times, to make himself visible to men, it is not proper at all to show the Holy Spirit as an adolescent or as a man since no where in the divine Scriptures do we discover that he appeared to men in such forms.

23. Coming back to the image we have been talking about [the Spirit in the form of a young man], it is not only quite

unusual, but it could, in addition, cause the people who look at it to fall again into an impious error condemned by the Fathers: the error of those who claimed that the divine Person of the Holy Spirit took on human nature.

24. This gives us the opportunity to make a second inquiry about whether it is proper to paint the Most Holy Trinity with colors. As much as it is possible, let us try to see which images of the Trinity are condemned, which other ones are not absolutely condemned, and which are the only ones approved and permitted.

25. It is a common opinion among theologians that it is permitted to paint the Most Holy Trinity with colors.

26. Nonetheless, it is absolutely excluded to allow painters to represent the Most Holy Trinity in any form whatsoever or according to their whims and boldness . . . .

27. Among the forbidden images of the Most Holy Trinity, we must unquestionably put . . . the Virgin Deipare . . . carrying the Trinity in her breast . . . .

28. As for the image consisting of one human body with three heads . . . , such images were solemnly condemned by our predecessor of blessed memory, Pope Urban VIII . . . who ordered the burning of certain paintings showing the Most Holy Trinity as a man with a triple face. This was done on August 11, 1628.

29. Let us now see what we ought to think about the image showing the Most Holy Trinity as three Persons, absolutely identical as to size, age, and features.

32. . . . the following are the commonly approved images of the Most Holy Trinity which can be permitted without any danger: 1) images which show the Person of God the Father in the form of an old man – as told in Daniel 7:9: 'and the one that was ancient of days took his seat' – with his only Son, Christ the God-Man, in his lap, and between the two of them the Holy Spirit in the form of a dove; 2) images which show two Persons separated by a small space, one being a man advanced in age, obviously the Father, and the other

Christ with the Holy Spirit in the form of a dove between them, as in the previous image . . . .

As for the first way of representing the Most Holy Trinity, especially the image showing Christ dead in the Father's lap, Molanus seems to hesitate in approving it on the grounds that nowhere do we read that Christ ever appeared dead to anyone. It is, however, easy to see that such an objection does not have much weight. Even though we nowhere read that our Lord ever appeared to anyone dead, it still remains that he died publicly and in full view of a large crowd. Why, then, should it be forbidden to paint him in the form in which he was seen in former times by so many thousands of people in Jerusalem, even if it is in the Father's lap? . . .

33.  . . . the best argument in favor of the image of the Holy Spirit in the form of a young man is found in the use of paintings showing the Most Holy Trinity as three identical Persons, . . . and the legitimacy of this usage is based on the appearance of three men to Abraham in Gn 18.

If the use of the corresponding image is not canonical, if the interpretation of the apparition as a prefiguration of the mystery of the Trinity is not guaranteed nor supported by solid proofs, then it is in no way permitted to maintain on such a fragile and doubtful basis, as though it were absolute fact, that it is legitimate to show the image of the Holy Spirit in the form of a man or a young man.

34.  Even if the painting of the Most Holy Trinity as three identical Persons were canonical, legitimate, and approved by the Church, and even if it were indisputable that the apparition of the three angels to Abraham were a prefiguration of the mystery of the adorable Trinity, the only thing we could infer from such facts is the legitimate and tolerable character of this way of representing the Trinity, that is, by three identical men with the same faces. In no way could we conclude, on the basis of these premises, that it is proper to represent the Holy Spirit as a man or a young man painted independently of the two other Persons. The apparition to Abraham was not just of one angel, but of three, and no where in the Holy Scriptures is it recorded that the Holy Spirit showed himself to men in the form of a man or a young man independently of the other . . . Persons of the Trinity.

36. The image of the Most Holy Trinity – of the Father, Son, and the Holy Spirit – is to be painted by representing either the Father beside the Son or the Son in the lap of the Father, along with the Holy Spirit each time, in the form of a dove, as we have stated before.

The Father can also be painted alone, independently of the other Persons because Adam heard the voice of the Lord God walking in Paradise . . . ; because he showed himself to Jacob on top of the mystical ladder . . . ; because he showed himself in an admirable way to Moses . . . , as well as to.Isaiah as the King seated on his throne . . . , and to Daniel as the old man clothed in a white garment . . . .

Equally, the eternal Son can be painted apart from the Father and the Holy Spirit because he became man, because he lived among men . . . It has also become customary to paint the Son as a lamb: the justification of this image is based on the prophecy of Isaiah and the witness of John the Baptist . . . .

The Holy Spirit, finally, can be painted either coming down from heaven in the form of tongues of fire on the day of Pentecost, or . . . in the form of a dove. Here also he is painted, alone, apart from the other divine Persons. Nowhere can we find the third Person appearing in the likeness of a man or of a young man apart from the two other Persons.[58]

## 26. Special Decrees of the Holy Synod of the Russian Church, 1722

*April 6, 1722:*

On the antimensia . . . , it is strictly forbidden to represent the Lord Sabaoth in the form of an old man, and the holy evangelists in the form of animals.[59]

Ouspensky:

. . . the special ruling of the Holy Synod of the Russian Church in 1722 . . . ordered that the image of God the Father on the antimensia be replaced by the inscription of the name of God in Hebrew, as a testimony to the divinity of Christ.[60]

*May 21, 1722:*

Ouspensky:

The second decree prohibited churches from owning icons carved on wood or sculpted in stone 'invented by inept or ill-intentioned iconographers.' Indeed, the decree stated, 'we do not have artists chosen by God. Only ignorant and ill-mannered people dare make such things. This custom has entered Russia through the agency of infidels, especially Romans and our neighbors, the Poles, who follow them.'

Aside from sculpture, the decree prohibited a whole series of icons 'contrary to nature, to history, and to truth itself . . . : the image of the Theotokos in labor during the Nativity of the Son, with a midwife next to her . . . ; the image of Florus and Laurus with horses and grooms bearing fictional names,' that is, traditional Orthodox subjects together with deviations.

Thus, the martyr St Christopher with the head of a dog; the Mother of God called 'with three hands,' no doubt with three natural hands instead of a pendentive; the image of the burning bush; 'the image of the Wisdom of God in the form of a young girl; the image of the creation of the world in six days by God, in which God is represented reclining on cushions . . . ; the image of Lord Sabaoth in the form of an elderly man with his only Son on his lap and between them the Holy Spirit in the form of a dove,' that is, the 'Paternity'; the Annunciation with the Father blowing from His mouth, a crucified cherubim, and so forth.[61]

## 27. The Decree of Catherine II, 1767

Ouspensky:

In 1767, Catherine II issued a decree prohibiting the painting of icons 'with unusual, scandalous features.' What she understood by this is not clear. We do, however, have some idea about her attitudes, because it was she who ordered that the iconostasis of Andrei Rublev be removed from the Cathedral of the Assumption in Vladimir, to be replaced by one in the Baroque style, with her own image on it as an icon of St Catherine.[62]

## 28. The Decree of the Holy Synod of Constantinople, 1776

Concerning the image of two men side by side with a dove between them, the so-called New Testament Trinity:

> It has been decreed by the Synod that the icon allegedly of the Trinity is an innovation. It is alien to the apostolic Orthodox Catholic Church and is not accepted by it. It infiltrated the Orthodox Church through the Latins.[63]

## 29. The Synod of Pistoie, Italy, September 18–28, 1786

Among the 57 articles issued by this synod, one required that images of the Trinity be taken out of the churches.[64]

## 30. Pope Pius VI, Auctorem fidei, August 28, 1794

In this encyclical of 85 propositions, the pope condemned the articles of the synod of Pistoie.

## 31. Decree of the Holy Synod of the Russian Church, Novmber 30, 1832

Ouspensky:

> The Synod promulgated a new decree forbidding statues. Numerous sculptures were destroyed as a result of this decree; others were hidden and then forgotten. The statues called 'Christ in prison,' preserved in great numbers in northern Russia, date back precisely to the eighteenth century. This subject appeared in the West at the end of the fifteenth century. Its best known example is an illustration of the Passion of Christ by Durer (called 'Kleine Passion'), where it is found on the cover. It had undoubtedly been imported to the north by Russian and foreign merchants through Arkhangelsk.[65]

## 32. Decision of the Holy Synod of the Russian Church, March 27 & April 14, 1880

In order that church painting, while faithfully preserving the tradition, may also meet the requirements of art and thereby exercise considerable influence on the development of an elegant taste in the masses, in addition to its religious significance, the Holy Synod views as very useful the mediation of the Imperial Academy of Fine Arts between the clients and the painters when iconostases, icons, and their frames are to be made.[66]

## 33. Decree of the Holy Synod of the Russian Church, 1888

Given the prejudice of the Old Ritualists against icons done in the new Italian style of painting, the parish priests must see to it that in Orthodox churches, especially in Old Ritualist areas, icons be close to the Greek originals in their painting.[67]

## 34. Pope Pius XII, Mediator Dei, November 20, 1947

The Adornment of Churches and Altars

189. . . . If we have previously disapproved of the error of those who would wish to outlaw images from churches on the plea of reviving an ancient tradition, We now deem it Our duty to censure the inconsiderate zeal of those who propose for veneration in the Churches and on the altars, without any just reason, a multitude of sacred images and statues, and also those who display unauthorized relics, those who emphasize special and insignificant practices, neglecting essential and necessary things. They thus bring religion into derision and lesson the dignity of worship.

The Other Arts in the Liturgical Cult

195. What We have said about music, applies to the other fine arts, especially to architecture, sculpture, and painting. Recent works of art which lend themselves to the materials of modern composition, should not be universally despised

and rejected through prejudice. Modern art should be given scope in the due and reverent service of the church and the sacred rites, provided that they preserve a correct balance between styles tending neither to extreme realism nor to excessive 'symbolism,' and that the needs of the Christian community are taken into consideration rather than the particular taste or talent of the individual artist. Thus modern art will be able to join its voice to that wonderful choir of praise to which have contributed, in honor of the Catholic faith, the greatest artists throughout the centuries. Nevertheless, in keeping with the duty of Our office, We cannot help deploring and condemning those works of art, recently introduced by some, which seem to be a distortion and perversion of true art and which at times openly shock Christian taste, modesty and devotion, and shamefully offend the true religious sense. They must be entirely excluded and banished from our churches, like 'anything else that is not in keeping with the sanctity of the place.'

196. Keeping in mind, Venerable Brethren, pontifical norms and decrees, take great care to enlighten and direct the minds and hearts of the artists to whom is given the task today of restoring or rebuilding the many churches which have been ruined or completely destroyed by war. Let them be capable and willing to draw their inspiration from religion to express what is suitable and more in keeping with the requirements of worship. Thus the human arts will shine forth with a wondrous heavenly splendor, and contribute greatly to human civilization, to the salvation of souls and the glory of God. The fine arts are really in conformity with religion when 'as noblest handmaids they are at the service of divine worship.'[68]

## 35. Directives of the French Episcopate: Episcopal Commission on Pastoral Relations and Liturgy: Some Guidelines about Sacred Art, April 28, 1952

Having been consulted on what is commonly called today 'the quarrel over sacred art,' the Episcopal Commission on Pastoral Relations and Liturgy felt it would be useful to set out clearly some guidelines that appear to be essential in this matter.

1.    As with any Art, and perhaps more so than any other, Sacred Art is, the Commission recognizes, 'living' and must correspond to the Spirit of its age, as well as to its technics and its materials.

2.    The Commission can only take great joy in the fact that contemporary artists, and among them some of the most famous, have been invited to work in our sanctuaries and have accepted to do so quite willingly.

3.    The Commission hopes that such artists will be able to assimilate the Christian spirit; otherwise, they will not be able to carry out their task properly. What work of Sacred Art can aspire to perfection in its genre without the inspiration of the Faith?

4.    Artists must also be convinced that when they are dealing with holy persons or religious subjects, they do not have the right to execute works containing deformations that might shock the faithful or that might give to the uninitiated the impression of being unworthy of the persons or mysteries represented, or even insulting to them. On this point, see the formal declaration made by the Sovereign Pontiff in November 1947 in the encyclical *Mediator Dei.*

5.    What is more, artists working in the sanctuaries must remember that they are not working in and for a closed circle of like-minded devotees. Consequently, their works must be understandable by all the faithful without having to make long and scholarly explanation. Church decorations will thus easily contribute to the edification and the education of the people who come to worship in the Holy Place, and, after all, that is how it should be. St. Thomas defined Beauty as '*quod visum placet.*'

6.    And finally, even though it is quite proper for a Christian critic to express freely his opinions on the quality of various works, which he has the right and the duty to judge, he should do so by respecting the directives of the hierarchy, the artists themselves, and other critics who may have other opinions . . . As the old saying goes . . . '*De gustibus et coloribus non est disputandum.*'

7. In addition, those who may find their works or themselves evaluated by a critic of Sacred Art must make an honest effort to understand what the critic, as well as anyone else, is saying.

8. In matters as complex and as delicate as Sacred Art, Christian critics, regardless of the point of view they represent, must always be very understanding and nuanced, must avoid absolute, offensive, and global judgments from which there is no appeal, and must try to bring into focus inspirations and expressions, especially in calm and tranquil conversations with other critics, artists, and persons who use their services.

9. Finally, the critic must always keep in mind that a new art, having more or less broken with old habits, can, in general, only be understood and appreciated from a certain distance in time and that a work of Art can only really be judged in the place where it is found, in its setting, in its own light. This is especially true of a decorative work.

10. The Commission naturally recognizes quite willingly that works of sugary sweet prettiness, which lack any life or nobility, must be increasingly kept away from our sanctuaries; unfortunately, such works far too often fill our churches, to our shame, moreover.

11. The Commission believes that the above is quite in line with the views expressed by the Sovereign Pontiff when he recommended that the bishops 'enlighten' the inspiration of artists (to whom will be assigned the restoration and the reconstruction of so many churches damaged or destroyed by the war) and that they guide the artists 'in the spirit and the direction of the pontifical guidelines.'

## 36. The Code of Canon Law of the Roman Catholic Church, 1983

*Canon 1188:*

The practice of displaying sacred images in the churches for the veneration of the faithful is to remain in force; nevertheless they are to be exhibited in moderate number and in suitable order lest they bewilder the Christian people and give opportunity for questionable devotion.

## Canon 1189:

Whenever valuable images, that is, those which are outstanding due to age, art, or cult, which are exhibited in churches or oratories for the veneration of the faithful need repair, they are never to be restored without the written permission of the ordinary who is to consult experts before he grants permission.

## Canon 1190:

1) It is absolutely forbidden to sell sacred relics.

2) Significant relics or other ones which are honored with great veneration by the people cannot in any manner be validly alienated or perpetually transferred without the permission of the Apostolic See.

3) The prescription of 2) is also applicable to images in any church which are honored with great veneration by the people."[69]

# NOTES

1  Bartlet, C., *Church-Life and Church-Order during the First Four Centuries* , Oxford, Blackwell, 1934, pp. 84 & 102-103.

2  Hippolytus of Rome, *The Apostolic Tradition* II, 11, Gregory Dix, ed., New York, The Macmillan Company, 1937, p. 25. I have italicized all the revelent passages.

3  Connolly, H., *Didascalia Apostolorum* , Oxford, Clarendon Press, 1929, pp. 156-158.

4  Harden, J. M., *The Ethiopic Didascalia* XXI, New York, Society for Promoting Christian Knowledge, 1920, pp. 101-102.

5  Nau, *La version syriaque de l'Octateuque de Clément* II, II,1, Paris, Lethielleux, reedited by Pio Ciprotti, 1967, pp. 57-58.

6  *Ibid.* VI, X, pp. 90-91.

7  Horner, G., *The Statues of the Apostles or Canones Ecclesiastici*, "Translation of the Saidic Text," 41: "Concerning the Occupations and the Crafts," London, 1904, p. 312.

8  *Ibid.*, "The Translation of the Arabic Text," 27: "Concerning the new persons . . . and the occupations which it is proper they should give up . . . ", p. 248.

9  *Patriologia Orientalis* XXXI, 2, *Les canons d'Hippolyte*, René-Georges Coquin, Paris, 1966, p. 365.

10  Hefele, J., *A History of the Councils of the Church* I, Edinburgh, T&T Clark, 1894, pp. 131-172, especially p. 151.

11  Kraeling, C., *The Christian Building, The Excavations at Dura-Europos: The Christian Building* , Final Report VIII-2, New Haven, Dura-Europos Publications, 1967, pp. 34-39.

12  Bovini, G., *I Sarcofagi paleocristiani della Spagna* , Rome, The Pontifical Institute of Christian Archaeology, 1954.

13  Laeuchli, S., *Power and Sexuality: The Emergence of Canon Law at the Synod of Elvira* , Philadelphia, Temple University Press, 1972, p. 36.

14  Gaudemet, J., "Le concile d'Elvire," *Dictionnaire d'Histoire de de Géographie Ecclésiastique* 15, 1963, col. 340-348.

15  *Livres des lettres* , Tiflis, 1901, pp. 72-77, in Sirarpie der Nersessian, "Une Apologie des Images du 7e siècle," *Byzantion* XVII, 1944-45, pp. 70-71; Vrej Nersessian, *The Tondrakian Movement* , Allison Park, Penn., Pickwick Publications, 1987, pp. 7-24.

16  *The Seven Ecumenical Councils* ,*The Nicene and Post-Nicene*

*Fathers* XIV, Eerdmans, 1979, p. 398.

17  *Ibid*, p. 401.

18  *Ibid*, p. 407.
    Hefele, *Councils* V, pp. 221-239.
    Ouspensky, L., *Theology of the Icon* I, Crestwood, N. Y., St. Vladimir's Seminary Press, 1992, pp. 91-100. This work is in two volumes, hereafter referred to as Ouspensky I or Ouspensky II.

19  Hefele, *Councils* V, pp. 301-302.

20  *Ibid*, p. 303.
    Ouspensky I, p. 110.

21  Anastos, M., "The Argument for Iconoclasm as Presented by the Iconoclastic Council of 754," *Late Classical and Medieval Studies in Honor of A. M. Friend, Jr.* , Princeton, 1954, pp. 185-187.
    Hefele, *Councils* V, pp. 307-317.
    Mango, C., *The Art of the Byzantine Empire 312-1453: Sources and Documents* , University of Toronto Press, 1986, pp. 165-68.
    Ouspensky I, pp. 119-150.

22  Hefele, *Councils* V, pp. 330-331.
    Leclercq, H., "Images (Culte et Querelle des)," *Dictionnaire d'Archéologie chrétienne et de Liturgie* I-2, col. 261-262.

23  Hefele, *Councils* V, p. 338.
    Lanne, E., "Rome et les saintes images," *Irénikon* 2, 1986, p. 172.
    Leclercq, col. 262-263.

24  Sahas, D., *Icon and Logos: Sources in Eighth century Iconoclasm*, Toronto, Ont., University of Toronto, 1986, pp. 176-180.
    Hefele, *Councils* V, pp. 342-393.
    Ouspensky I, pp. 119-150.

25  Hefele, *Histoire des Conciles* III-2, Paris, p. 1056, hereafter referred to as *Conciles* and not to be confused with the English translation *Councils*. This is my English translation from the French edition; the five-volume English translation of Hefele does not go beyond the 7th Ecumenical Council of 787.

26  See Hefele, *Conciles* III-2, p. 1068

27  Ouspensky I, p. 143.

28  Mango, pp. 168-169.
    Alexander, J. P., "The Iconoclastic Council of St. Sophia (815) and Its Definition (Horos)," *Dumbarton Oaks Papers* 7,

1953, pp. 35-66.

29  Hefele, *Conciles* IV-1, pp. 43-49.
    Ouspensky I, pp. 143-144.

30  Hefele, *Conciles* IV-1, p. 272 ff.

31  Ouspensky II, p. 212.
    Hefele, *Conciles* IV-1, p. 522.

32  Ouspensky II, note 20, p. 215.
    Hefele, *Conciles* IV-1, p. 524.

33  Ouspensky II, p. 263.
    Kazakova, N. A. and Ia. S. Lourié, *The Heretical, Antifeudal Movements in Russia from the 14th century to the Beginning of the 16th Century* (in Russian), Moscow-Leningrad, 1955, p. 383.

34  Hautecoeur, l., "Le Concile de Trente et l'art," *Il Concilio di Trento e la ariforma tridentina* , *Atti del Convegno storico internazionale* (September 1965), p. 346.

35  Duchesne, E., *Le Stoglav ou les cent chapitres* , Bibliothèque de l'Institut français de Pétrograd, Paris, Librairie Ancienne Honoré Champion, 1920, pp. 27-28. Hereafter referred to as Duchesne.

36  Duchesne, pp. 82-83.          37  Ouspensky II, p. 291.

38  Ouspensky II, p. 290.

39  Duchesne, pp. 111-112.
    Ouspensky II, p. 290.

40  Duchesne, pp. 133-135.        41  Ouspensky II, p. 300

42  Duschesne, p. 135            43  Ouspensky, p. 300

44  Duchesne, p. 133-135         45  Ouspensky II, p. 300

46  Duschesne, p. 135            47  Ouspensky II, p. 300

48  Duchesne, p. 136             49  Ouspensky II, pp. 293-294

50  Duchesne, p. 136             51  Duchesne, p. 209

52  Ouspensky II, pp. 303-323.

53  *The Canons and Decrees of the Council of Trent* , T. Buckley, tr., London, Routledge, 1851, pp. 213-215.

54  Latin text in *Mansi* 35, 1330.
    English text in James Hough, *History of Christianity in India*, vol. II, R. B. Seeley and W. Burnside, London, 1839, p. 661.
    J. Thaliath, "The Synod of Diamper," *Orient Christiana Analecta*, 152, Rome, 1958.

55  Bœsplug, F., *Dieu dans l'art* , Paris, Editions du Cerf, 1984, p. 43.

56 Ouspensky II, pp. 371-372; for an analysis, see pp. 372-409.

57 Le Bachelet, "Alexandre VIII," *Dictionnaire de Théologie Catholique* 1-1, col. 747-763.

58 Boespflug, F., *Dieu dans l'art* , Paris, Editions du Cerf, 1984, pp. 22-59.

59 Ouspensky II, note 19, p. 380

60 Ouspensky II, p. 380 & p. 415
*The Complete Collection of the Decisions of the Department of the Orthodox Confession* (in Russian), vol 2, Decision no. 516, pp. 163-164.

61 Ouspensky II, (note 16), pp. 415-16.
*The Complete Collection of the Decisions of the Department of the Orthodox Confession* (in Russian), vol 2, Decision no. 516, pp. 293-295.

62 Ouspensky II, p. 425.

63 Sethad, *Bibliotheca graeca mediiaevi* , vol. 3, Venice, 1872, p. 317.
Ouspensky II, pp. 397-398.

64 *Dictionnaire des conciles* , M. Minge, ed., Paris, 1847, col. 405-407.
*Dictionnaire de Théologie Catholique* 12-2.

65 Ouspensky II, note 15, pp. 415-416.

66 Bulgakov, S. *The Clergy Manual* (in Russian), Kiev, 1913, see note, p. 746.
Ouspensky II, pp. 437-438.

67
Bulgakov, S. *The Clergy Manual* (in Russian), Kiev, 1913, p. 742.
Ouspensky II, note 75, p. 438.

68 Pope Pius XII, "Mediator Dei," *The Papal Encyclicals 1939-1958* , Raleigh, N. C., McGrath, 1981, pp. 148-150.

69 *The Code of Canon Law: A Text and Commentary* , J. Coriden et al, eds., London, Chapman, 1984, p. 841.

*Fig. 30*

*Fig. 31*

# The Not-So-Penetrating Look

## The Problem

Have you ever noticed that on certain icons, the persons depicted, though they seem to be looking at you, are in fact looking away from you? (*fig. 30*) Christ, the Mother of God, or the saints have their faces turned directly to the viewer, but, either slightly or very obviously, they are not engaging in eye-to-eye contact. (*fig. 31*) I am not referring, to feastal and other event-oriented icons, for example, that of the Forty Martyrs of Sebaste, whose purpose is principally to make present persons "in-an-event." Icons, such as those of the Mother of Tenderness, the Deisis, or St John the Theologian in meditation, though they are person-oriented, are not strictly intended to draw us into a direct personal communion with the persons depicted.

Are the saints in some icons avoiding eye contact by accident or on purpose? Do iconographers paint them this way for a reason? If so, what reason? Whether icons are painted this way by accident or on purpose, the question of eye contact in icons is an important one.

## Psychological Background

About an hour later another man insisted saying, "This fellow was certainly with him. Why, he is a Galilean." "My friend," said Peter, "I do not know what you are talking about." At that instant while he was still speaking, the cock crew, and the Lord turned and looked straight at Peter, and Peter remembered what the Lord had said to him, "Before the cock crows today, you will have disowned me three times." And he went outside and wept bitterly. (St. Luke 22:60-62)

From this passage, and from our own experience, we know the importance and power of a look: "If looks could kill. . . ." In everyday life, eye contact is a vehicle for so much communication; it accompanies verbal as well as non-verbal communication. A public speaker can live or die through eye contact. We are ill at ease when certain people look us right in the eye; we sense the presence of someone or something we do not want to be close to. Lovers penetrate into each other by prolonged eye contact. It is commonplace that the eyes are a gateway into the soul, into the mystery that is the human person. We not only receive others into ourselves through our eyes, but we also display ourselves to others in the same way. Our eyes are like a TV screen onto which we project our inner selves. If eye contact with another person is broken for some reason or purposefully avoided, we immediately feel a loss of contact, a loss of presence, and communication is impeded. Nothing is more unnerving than for someone to speak to us and never look us straight in the eye. Have you ever talked to someone wearing sun glasses?

## DOCTRINAL BACKGROUND

[A man who robbed churches confesses ...] Once I broke into a church where there was a miraculous icon. I went up to this image in order to take advantage of what I thought would be an easy take. At that moment, I looked at the Christ-Child and was glued to the floor, petrified. A few minutes later I tried again to extend my hand toward the image but for the second time, the Christ-Child paralyzed me by his look. Oh well, I thought, a bungled job. . . . [1]

In his book *The Art of the Icon: A Theology of Beauty*, Paul Evdokimov has a chapter on the "Theology of Presence." In this and other chapters, the author sets out what we know to be one of the purposes of Orthodox icons, namely to make present the person or persons represented in the image. The person's presence in his image is at the heart of the theological vision which undergirds the Orthodox Church's experience of icons. Among other things, we read in many sources that the eyes of the saints painted on icons are larger than in natural life so as to emphasize that personal presence which is carried by and through the eyes. *(figures 32 and 33)* Other artistic techniques, such as inverse perspective, are used to enhance the feeling that the persons painted in icons are looking at us, addressing us, and penetrating us by their looks. How many people do not like icons or do not want to look at them, not for æsthetic reasons, but because they are unnerved by the penetrating look of holiness coming at them through the saints' eyes? And this is, of course, the whole purpose of those penetrating looks: to draw our attention to the impurities, sins, and darkness in us, move us to repentance and purification, and open us up to that transfiguring communion which is the Kingdom of God.

## THE PROBLEM FOCUSED

It goes without saying, then, that in those icons whose purpose it is to create immediate personal communion between us (the looked-at-ones) and the saints (the looking-ones), eyes that do not look at us are an obvious obstacle to the achieving of the icon's basic purpose. *(fig. 34)* Such icons as the Pantocrator, Hodigitria, individual or grouped saints, ought to look us in the eye, directly and obviously, so as to penetrate us with their transfiguring looks. When, for one reason or another, the saint's eyes are turned horizontally from a straight on look,

*Fig. 32*

*Fig. 33*

*Fig. 34*

*Fig. 35*

Fig. 36

Fig. 37

Fig. 38

Fig. 39

*Fig. 40*

*Fig. 41*

when his head is turned 45° from the direct frontal position (fig. 35), or when he is looking up to heaven in a "pious" stare, then communion is lost or greatly diminished. (fig. 36)

This is evident in certain Hodigitria icons (fig. 37): the Mother of God is "showing us the way" by her hand gesture, but her eyes look elsewhere. Christ blesses us, but does not look at us. The same phenomenon is apparent in certain icons of bishops or priests who, while blessing us, look off to the side. (fig. 38)

It may be said that these "off-in-the-distance" looks of some saints are meant to emphasize their ministry of intercession before God. (figs. 39-41) They look at God on our behalf. It is true, of course, that the saints are our intercessors and that the honor given to the image rises to the prototype, but the purpose of an icon is not to show the saint in intercession but rather to show us the saint in the Kingdom of God and thereby to be a conduit of grace for us. The primary line of vision is "us-ward": from the person in the Kingdom through the icon to us.

What are the reasons for the saints' averted looks, for reducing the power of their penetrating glance? Are we to assume lack of talent, sentimentality, lack of knowledge, bad models, etc? Perhaps the most important thing is simply to draw our attention to the theological and psychological significance of eyes that look directly at us in our iconographic tradition. We thereby strengthen the power of Christ to change people's lives through the penetrating look of icons.

# NOTES

1 Archimandrite Spiridon, *Mes missions en Sibérie* [My Missions in Siberia], Paris: Cerf, 1968, p. 84.

# DEATH AND ORTHODOX ICONOGRAPHY

## INTRODUCTION

In the Orthodox Church, iconography holds a central and important place, both visually and theologically. Icons are not merely decorations or pictorial teaching aides. They do serve these purposes, but their fundamental reason for being is to bear witness, in an artistic manner, to the Church's beliefs. They are a reflection of the life in Christ as lived in the Church. We should expect, therefore, to receive from iconography that which is witnessed to and preached by other means, such as Scripture, liturgical texts, dogmatic statements, and the writings of the Fathers.

The subject of death, especially Christian death, is certainly an important one. In some ways, it is the central problem not only of Christian living but also of all human existence. What is death, and why do we die? The Church certainly has answers to these questions which are not isolated. In fact, they touch on the whole structure of Church doctrine. It is only natural, then, to expect to see the Church's beliefs about death reflected in her iconography. The question is how to "read out" of icons the doctrinal content that has already been "read in to" them. The purpose of this paper is to examine the ways death is portrayed in Orthodox iconography. We plan first to deal briefly with the doctrines of death and icons, then generally with death in icons. Then we will move on to the specific ways death is depicted, and finally we will consider the differences between Eastern and Western iconographies of death.

## THE DOCTRINE OF SALVATION

Implicit in the word salvation is a notion of what we are saved from. For every salvation, there is a lostness; for every liberty, a slavery. We need to have an idea of what the Church sees as the opposite of salvation, what we are saved from. Without much question, death is the concept and the reality which is identified by the Church as the great enemy, the great destroyer, and it is from the clutches of death that we are to be saved. Death – the inevitability of every person's dying – is tied up closely with sin. St. Paul states that, "the wage paid by sin is death" (Rom 6:23). Death is seen, then, as the result of something else; it is the result of man's subjugation to a power that seeks his enslavement and destruction. The opposite of Christian salvation is the enslavement of sin which results in death. Sin itself, however, does not arise outside of man; it is not a power that is imposed on him by an alien master. Ironically, it is man himself who is the author of his own slavery and destruction. By turning away from the author of his being toward himself, man is cut off from the source of his own life, and so he withers and dies.

All creation came into existence out of nothing, absolute non-being. To the degree that we do not rise to and bask in the light of Him who created us, we sink slowly back into that abyss of nothingness out of which we came. Death is a powerful thrust downward into that black pit, leading to decomposition not only of the body but also of the whole man. Man is not to be defined as a soul living in a body, two or more natural substances which happen, for a while, to be joined together so that death is the separation of man from his body. According to this idea, man is essentially identified with a soul. Such a view, however, is not Christian. For Christianity, man is a unitary, though composite, being who is in touch with and allied to many aspects of reality: the physical world through his body, the intellectual world through his mind, the spiritual world through his heart or soul. There is no natural line of demarcation whereby the mind, body, soul, heart, emotions, etc. peel off from each other like layers of an onion. A man is not fully man if deprived of his properties and faculties created by God. Death, in this view, is a radical ripping apart of man's composite being. It tears apart his being, somewhat like a bee whose insides are pulled out when it stings: in death, man as an entity decomposes. It is only as the Christian man carries within himself the new humanity of Christ that he is given the chance to overcome the present human condition and attain salvation in the midst of this world and beyond it.

It is here that we move from the description of the present, deathbound condition of man to the envisioned salvation. For Orthodox Christianity, the important word in defining salvation is transfiguration, the changing of the conditions by which man lives. This means not only the transformation of man himself, but also the environment in which he lives. The whole of creation needs to be changed and transfigured so as to eliminate the hold sin and death have on the world. We cannot effect this transfiguration by ourselves; we are powerless to change our condition. Therefore, our salvation requires an intervention from outside our world. Christ's life and work are that intervention. He came into our world, broke the power of sin and death, and made it possible for us to live in a different way than the fallen nature of man requires. By being turned toward the source of our being instead of away from it, we can live rather than die. Christ created a new type of humanity, or more precisely, He restored the old humanity to what it should have been in the first place. By uniting ourselves to His new humanity in the Church and by being nourished by His life in the holy mysteries, we can transform and transfigure our present fallen condition so that death will have no final power over us. This re-creation of man and the world in their final state is called the Kingdom of God. By our progressive transfiguration, we participate in the building up of the Kingdom until its final establishment in the new heaven and the new earth where the present conditions of death, sin, and decay will no longer be operative. We will then live the life of intimate communion with God that we were meant to live from the beginning.

One of the key terms used to designate the transfigured world growing now within the Church is the "new Jerusalem." In his vision recorded in Revelation, St. John the Theologian describes what the Kingdom of God will be like when Christ comes again in glory:

> Then I saw a new heaven and a new earth; for the first heaven and the first earth had passed away. . . . I saw the holy city, new Jerusalem, coming down out of heaven from God, prepared as a bride adorned for her husband. . . . "Behold the dwelling of God is with men. . . . He will wipe away every tear from their eyes, and death shall be no , neither shall there be mourning nor crying nor pain any more, for the former things have passed away.... He who sat upon the throne said, "Behold, I make all things new..." (Rev 21:1-5)

Here we see very clearly the idea of the transformation of the old fallen world into the new one of which we have a foretaste in the Church, but which will only come in fullness at the end of time, on the Eighth Day of re-creation.

St. Paul, too, emphasizes this distinction between the old and the new man, life according to the old Adam and life according to the new Adam, who is Christ. In our baptism we die to the old, fallen man, and reclothe ourselves in Christ. We take on the new life of the Kingdom and live anew in that reality while still in the midst of the old. To quote St. Paul again: "It is no longer I who live, but Christ who lives in me." (Gal 2:20) So when we die the death of this world, it is the old man that dies. But for who die in Christ, have another life within themselves, Christ's life, His new humanity, and so, though dead, they are alive in Him.

How, then, does iconography relate to this concept of a progressive transfiguration into the new creation? Icons portray the new creation (the new Jerusalem, the Kingdom of God, the new humanity, etc.) in artistic form. This is the primary function of Orthodox iconography, and iconography is true to its purpose only to the degree that it draws us out of this world and its conditions and transports us into the new world which is to come. That is why no attempt is made in icons to reflect the so-called natural world, a world that is precisely not natural because it is fallen. Icons do not depict proportion, depth, three dimensions, etc. because these things are proper to this world and not to the re-creation of the Kingdom. Iconography has its own symbolic language and techniques which have been developed and adapted so as to portray in the most vivid way the transfigured, spiritual world and the men and women who inhabit it. Kalokyris puts the point well:

> The faith of the Church in the reality beyond this world, that is, in the truth of the spiritual world, defined from the begin-

ning the essential character of the content of her iconography. She is primarily interested in the beauty of this spiritual world, and with the means which she possesses, the Church seeks to be the interpreter of that world.[1]

From the foregoing, then, how should we expect death to be portrayed in icons? If death is part of this old world which is passing away and if icons show that world which is to come, we can expect that death will not be portrayed in them at all. This is precisely the point we wish to make: death as a phenomenon is absent from iconography, but at the same time, it is ever-present. As the Reformation only makes sense if contrasted with medieval Catholicism, or the communist revolution if contrasted with the czarist state, so iconography only makes sense if we assume the presence behind and beneath it of the old world out of which the new creation arises.[2] Death is ever-present by its absence, its banishment, since it has been conquered by Christ and eliminated as a power. But because we are now living in the interim before the full establishment of the Kingdom, in the period when the new and old creations still exist together, death is sometimes represented in iconography, but only in a vanquished, powerless, and empty form. It is as though it were making a final appearance in chains before being totally destroyed. This, then, is what we want to set out: the vanquished character of death as shown in icons.

## GENERAL CONSIDERATIONS

The first place we need to look for a demonstration of the omnipresence of death by its omni-absence is in the catacomb art of the pre-Constantinian Church. Here we have a definitely funereal art. The context in which the art appears could not be more death-centered, and yet in the art itself there is no representation of the dead as such, no symbolized death, nothing to recall this deathbound world. In the midst of dead things, in the place of the dead, the art calls the viewer to think of deliverance and life:

> Thus, for example, the oldest symbol, that of a ship: to the man of the Græco-Roman antiquity, it had suggested the voyage of souls into the beyond, but by the time of the Empire, it came to mean a happy passage through life; it was only a sign of prosperity, with the end of the voyage representing death. Christians, taking up the symbol and restoring its primitive meaning, transformed it into a symbol of the faith of the Church and of the soul which the Church guides. . . . The arrival of the ship to the harbor had signified the end: death. For a Christian, on the contrary, it implied the entrance of the soul into eternal repose and bliss. The pessimistic outlook of the pagan was replaced by the joyous confidence in the resurrection.[3]

Why is it that for the early Christians there is no sign of death, no figure of death, no picture of the dead as dead? Even though the pictures are surrounded by the final reality of this world, the faith of these Christians that their loved ones were alive in Christ, although dead in this world, was so strong as to eliminate any trace of that dead world from their very earliest art:

> The art of the catacombs is not only a funereal art and does not only consist in symbolic and allegorical representations as is sometimes thought to be the case. Of course, it does include many funereal elements, but it is above all an art which teaches the faith. . . . In the first century, these [symbols and images] consist of the Good Shepherd, Noah and the ark, Daniel in the lions' den, and the banquet scene. In the second century, there are many images from the New Testament: the annunciation, the nativity of Christ, His baptism and others.[4]

What is striking is that these scenes depict acts of deliverance. God acts to save those in trouble. As He acted to save and deliver the saints of old, so He acts to save

171

those who die in Christ. The New Testament scenes thus depict Christ's life, the act of deliverance par excellence.

Another area where we might expect to find death and dying vividly depicted is in connection with martyrdom. Today, we want to know the details of a new martyr's death. The same interest was also prevalent in the early Church, as the various written martyrologies testify. But when it comes to the depiction of the martyrs themselves, we are no longer concerned with how they died; that is really unimportant. What we need to see depicted is their glorified state in the Kingdom. With persecution a constant possibility, and physical death always near for those who followed Christ, why is it that earthly reality is not reflected in the catacomb art? Only artistic expressions of the hope of deliverance, of resurrection to the new creation, are seen:

> Thus no trace of the frequent persecutions and the numerous martyrs of this time can be found in the liturgical art of the catacombs. The Christian artist . . . undoubtedly saw the atrocious scenes of the amphitheaters . . . and one would expect to see recollections of these days when the struggle of the Christians against the pagan gods reached its paroxysm. But not one scene of martyrdom can be found in the catacombs. . . . It is only later when the persecutions had ceased and the anguish of the Christians had become history that they were sometimes represented.[5]

The representation of the Martyrs of Sebaste is an example of this.[6]

The dead person, perhaps a martyr, is often seen in the orant position, the hands lifted up in prayer. Having died in Christ and for Christ, that is his essential condition: praying in the Kingdom for those left behind, but who are soon to follow. "The drama of the represented situation is not so much the very moment of sacrifice as the internal spiritual state of the person, i. e. the state of prayer."[7] Thus in the first stage of Christian art, funereal though it was, there was no place for "natural" death to be represented.

## SPECIFIC EXAMPLES

One of the primary symbolic representations of death, or the realm of the dead, in iconography is darkness, a black area on an icon. Darkness as a symbol of night runs throughout the Bible and the writings of the Fathers, so it is natural that Satan's kingdom should be represented by black. Evdokimov puts it this way:

> ...the prologue of the fourth gospel: "The light shines in the darkness." The absolute polarity that this passage contains requires us to understand "darkness" in its ultimate, hellish sense as a designation for all that tragically went wrong with God's plan throughout human history. Seen from the point of view of time, the child in the cave is the most distressing coexistence of Light and darkness, of God and Satan. . . . Seen from the point of view of eternity, . . . "the Sun which set with him dissipated the darkness of death forever. . . ."[8]

One specific way that this kingdom of darkness is shown is by a cave opening to the inner earth, the underground, which is the symbolic realm of the dead and of Satan. The icons of the Nativity, the Myrrh-bearing Women, the Crucifixion, the Raising of Lazarus, the Descent into Hell, and others depict dark caverns. The icon of Theophany pictures the dark river Jordan, which is sometimes made to look like a lake but nevertheless represents a dark, bottomless pit. The icon of Pentecost places the old man Cosmos in a dark area at the bottom of the icon: Cosmos, the world, is in the midst of Satan's kingdom. In all of these icons, however, the dark area is not represented as an independent reality but is only the stage for reception of the new creation. It is into this darkness that Christ or His light now shines. As stated above, when death or its kingdom appear in icons, it is only to show that their power is broken, they wait to be filled with Christ's life. Thus in the scene of the Nativity, Christ is lying in a manger in a dark cave with the light of the star shining down upon it.[9]

In some, though not all, icons of the Myrrh-bearing Women,[10] one of the angels of light is seated in the dark tomb. On the Good Friday icon, the cross stands above a cave on Golgotha. Lazarus, "prefiguring the general resurrection", also emerges from a darkened tomb. Christ at His baptism is submerged in the dark kingdom of the Jordan, recreating water, turning what had been an instrument of death into an instrument of life:

> Water changes its meaning. Formerly it was an image of death, the Flood, but now it has become "the well of the water of life." . . . The liturgy calls non-sanctified water "a liquid tomb," *hydatostratos taphos*, as the image of death-flood. In fact, the icon shows Jesus going down into the waters as into a watery tomb. The Jordan is in the form of a dark cave, the iconographic image for Hades; it contains the Lord's entire body, as an image of burial.[11]

In icons of the Descent into Hell, in addition to Christ's being in the dark pit, we often find Satan or death represented as a chained man lying amidst the locks and keys of the broken gates of hell. On the Pentecost icon, the fire of the Holy Spirit descends on the old man, Cosmos, in the black pit of this unregenerated world, through the apostles who represent the Church. The evangelists may be depicted as writing in a dark cave, an image of the present world about to receive the Gospel.[12] In these and other cases, the dark area is in the lower part of the icon, representing openings into the lower world, into which salvation comes from above.

This symbolism of darkness is also reflective of the doctrine that evil, death, and sin are not created realities in themselves; they are negations of created good things. They always move toward destruction and the nothingness out of which all creation came, and away from the full being which is God. Iconography stresses this antimanichean belief about the contingent nature of evil. Only God exists; only His light and power give being. To turn away from that source is to slide into the black pit of death and nothingness. We can either rise toward the source of our life, represented at the top of the icons, or slide down to our destruction represented at the bottom.

We need to look also at the representation of death by symbolic skulls and bones. The basic principle continues to hold true: there are very few such representations because a skeleton represents death and the fallen condition of this present life. However, we do often find a skull in the cave beneath the cross on the Good Friday icon.

> In a Christian tradition, Golgotha is the center of the world. There Adam was created and buried, and there the Cross was raised up. We often see Adam's tomb and skull represented at the foot of the Cross. . . . This is a very frequent subject in icons. . . .[13] This is why on the icons, the foot of the cross goes down into a black cavern in which we see Adam's head, Golgotha being the "place of the skull" (Jn 19:17). This symbolic detail shows the head of the first Adam, and in him all human beings are washed by Christ's blood.[14]

But Adam's skull, representing the death of the first man, is shown only in relation to the death of the New Man who destroyed death itself.

There are other icons in which bones and skulls appear, but seemingly only for artistic effect and not as the departure point for a theology of redemption: for example, the Last Judgment and the Valley of Dry Bones.[15] Neither subject is of major iconographic import; nonetheless, they exist.

Tombs are another specific symbol of death and serve as the background out of which comes life. In the icon of the Raising of Lazarus, a coffin is sometimes shown in the cave; at other times, the cave itself is the tomb. In this image, Lazarus is being raised again to this present life and not to the new and unending life of the Kingdom. In the Church's understanding, this event, celebrated on the Saturday before Holy Week, is a prefiguration of Christ's and our own resurrection. The Descent into Hell shows Adam and Eve being raised out of their tombs by Christ into the new life. The image of the Myrrh-bearing Women shows only a tomb, without the body. Again we see that the old death, with its normal setting and customary characteristics, has been left behind.

Next let us look at the way the dead are represented immediately following their death. The Crucifixion, the Epitaphion, and the Dormition icons are our main examples. Even though the Crucifixion depicts Jesus as dead, the Church sees His death as a victory: to show forth perfect humanity in obedience to the Father's will, Christ maintained His integrity even in the face of death. The icon depicts Him with His eyes closed and His expression calm and peaceful. Victory and peace in the worst of deaths are expressed by the position of the body and its general appearance:

> In the East, the icon of the crucified Christ never shows the realism of exhausted and dead flesh; painful expressions of agony have no place. Dead and at peace, Christ loses nothing of his royal nobility and always keeps his majesty.[16]

The same can be said for the icon of the Epitaphion

venerated on Good Friday and Holy Saturday. Christ is dead and in the tomb; yet no corruption or decomposition is shown, evidence of the hollow and illusory victory won by Satan at the Crucifixion.

The Dormition provides an interesting contrast to the Crucifixion. Mary lies dead upon the bier, yet she is alive, like a little child, in the arms of Christ who stands behind her. In death, she is portrayed as old and at peace, as though asleep. She is surrounded by the Church, represented by the apostles and other members of the earthly community, together with angels and Christ who receives her. What a perfect depiction of the Christian idea of death in the Lord: no longer black, dark, and cold; no longer filled with fear, pain, and separation, but calm and full of light, surrounded by Christ and His Body the Church. Would that each Christian's death could be like hers! The Dormition icon thus offers a perfect representation of one of the Church's petitions: "A Christian ending to our life, painless, blameless, peaceful, and a good defense before the dread judgment seat of Christ, let us ask of the Lord."

We should remember that the dead often appear in icons of events that occur subsequent to their deaths. This is especially true of Old Testament figures. In the Transfiguration icon, we see Moses and Elijah who represent both the dead and the living of the Old Testament. While Moses' death is recorded in Scripture, Elijah does not die a natural death but is taken directly by God in a flaming chariot. All the figures in the icon of the Descent into Hell, David, Solomon, Moses, John the Baptist, etc. have already died; yet they are alive as they view the "future" event of Adam and Eve's resurrection. Similarly, any icon of an apparition of Christ, of the Theotokos or of a saint in Church history depicts the person who has died and is yet alive. Iconography proclaims that those who have died in the Lord are in fact alive, in contrast to those who are still alive, but who in Christ are dead to the old world.

Let us turn briefly to the way icons are displayed in the church building. Classically the church is constructed in three sections: the sanctuary, the nave, and the narthex.[17] The sanctuary represents the heaven of heavens where Christ the King rules over all. The nave is the place of the new creation and the Kingdom of God. Christ the Pantokrator is painted in the dome of the nave to show His rule in the Kingdom. The narthex, finally, illustrates the realm of this world that opens back into the darkness, just as it opens into the light of the Kingdom. It is appropriate that icons and frescoes in the nave and in the sanctuary should illustrate the defeat of the kingdom of death. As we enter from the outside, we begin to see the new world where death has no place. Since the Kingdom of God is to come fully only after the end of time, it is appropriate to represent the Last Judgment on the western wall of the narthex. To reach the fullness of the Kingdom, we must all pass through this judgment. What we have experienced partially in the Church as judgment and sanctification is thus represented in the organization and symbolism of the church building itself. Therefore, both the content of icons and their location within the church building teach us that, for the Christian, death is a thing of the past, both literally and symbolically behind us.

## EASTERN AND WESTERN ART

Here we would like to make a few observations concerning the evident differences between Orthodox iconography and Western religious paintings. The differences are striking, even to the most casual observer. If our basic premise is correct, namely that religious art expresses a particular understanding of reality, then we should be able to understand some of the theological differences between the two traditions by observing how these two types of art treat the theme of death.

The Orthodox Church claims that its theology of death and its art forms are continuous with the earliest manifestations of Christian art in the catacombs. Iconography shows a great stability and regularity in its inspiration and execution throughout the centuries. During the first thousand years of Christian history, Latin religious art generally represented a variation of this same tradition. Philippe Ariès, in his book *The Hour of Our Death*, makes the claim that Western art for about the first millennium, up to and including the Romanesque period, reflected the theology of death prevalent at that time:

> Let us begin by recalling what was said . . . about the Christians of the first millennium. They believed that after their death they rested like the Seven Sleepers of Ephesus, awaiting the day of Christ's return. Their image of the end of time was that of the glorified Christ as he rose to heaven on the day of Ascension or . . . as he is described by the visionary of the Book of Revelations. . . . This extraordinary imagery recurs again and again in the Romanesque period. . . . On those rare occasions when funerary art did represent the Last Judgment, it is apparent that the event inspired very little fear since it was consistently seen from the point of view of the return of Christ and the awakening of the just. . . . This is the traditional image that is repeated in Romanesque art. . . .[18]

On a baptismal font found in France, dating no later than 1150, we have the following scene of the Resurrection:

The risen souls are emerging naked from their sarcophagi in pairs, husband and wife embracing. . . . The relation between baptism and resurrection is clear. Those who have been baptized were assured of resurrection and their eternal salvation it implied.[19]

The spirit here expressed is very close to the Orthodox ethos. The techniques also are very similar to the Byzantine: "We know that the Carolingian and Romanesque artist employed a perspective that was different from that of the viewer: he showed the viewer what he could not see, as he ought to see it."[20] It is clear that in this period both East and West were drinking from the same fountain of inspiration.

It is part of Ariès' general thesis, however, that something in the West during the eleventh and twelfth centuries began to change on the level of feelings and deep-seated psychology. This change began to manifest itself in a funerary art very different from what had gone before. The result was a total divergence of the new Western religious art in both inspiration and technique from Orthodox iconography, which continued in the traditional path. Western art moved in a this-worldly direction to concentrate on life as lived here and now and to measure it in terms of immanent factors. Thus, art itself moved toward representing the so-called natural world as we see it, and away from symbolic representations. Ariès is not the only one to see this change and to comment on it:

But starting in the thirteenth century, Giotto, Duccio, and Cimabue introduced into their works optical illusion, perspective, depth, chiaroscuro [play of light and shadows], and trompe-l'œil [still-life deception]. Such art, though more refined and more reflective of the natural world, lost the ability to directly grasp and portray the transcendent. . . . Having broken with the artistic canons of tradition, western Christian art could no longer be integrated into the liturgical mystery, and having left its heavenly "biosphere," it became more and more autonomous and subjective.[21]

The empirical world became the real world and, therefore, the appropriate world to copy in art. As far as religious painting was concerned, two trends appeared: 1) religious subjects became only the occasion for the artist to express himself; there was no essential difference in inspiration or technique between a religious, mythological, secular, or even pornographic subject. 2) Religious subjects were painted in the most realistic style, reflective of the way the event may actually have looked. The new realism was expressed in both physical and psychological terms, in the striving for the accurate depiction of clothing, anatomy and furniture as well as the convincing portrayal of agony, pain or suffering. The point was that religious art tried to reflect as much as possible an actual scene as imagined by the artist.

Ironically, the "realism" of the new style proved less and less capable of fulfilling the function of traditional religious art: to facilitate communion between the viewer and the religious subject - i.e., God. Thus Archimandrite Vasilios writes:

> What a disappointment, what a temptation to unbelief you find the approach to Christ "according to man": seeing Christ in the flesh, depicting Him in a painting as an ordinary man of His time, thinking that you will come nearer to the truth about Him the more faithfully you manage to copy the landscape of Palestine or present the area as it was at that period.[22]

In Western art, there were, of course, symbolic and allegorical paintings as well as other art forms depicting lambs, angels, God the Father, and so on. But again, they were executed in terms of the "natural" world in which the artist lived. Consequently, as epochs and styles changed, so did the artistic renderings of religious subjects.

The ramifications of this fundamental change in outlook concerning artistic representations of death were enormous. Ariès chronicles the results of this and other changes by showing in exhaustive detail the upsurge in interest in scenes of death, various means of death, pain, suffering leading to death, and dead and decaying bodies. Through a full six hundred pages, he presents the seemingly infinite variety of artistic representations of death, from tombs decorated with sculptures of decaying bodies to later depictions of death related to eroticism.

Such depictions are not surprising where the purpose of art is understood to be the representation of the natural order. Death is a part of this world; consequently, decomposing flesh is as proper a subject for expression as roses in spring. It all becomes a matter of taste.

Such an attitude toward art and artistic expression could not be farther from the Orthodox understanding of death and of its depiction in iconography. Unfortunately however, Orthodox theology, as well as its artistic theory and expression, have been seriously infiltrated by the very ideas, psychology, and techniques which have run unrestrained in the West. So serious is this problem that it is no exaggeration to say that in many Orthodox churches built in the ninteenth and early twentieth centuries, there are few if any icons at all. There may be many religious paintings, but real icons are few. That this tendency did not totally corrupt the Church can only be attributed to the strong, unconscious sense of the true purpose of icons within Orthodoxy. Kalokyris put it this way:

We attribute this fact not to the intentions . . . but to the false ideas about art, according to which an icon or a wall-painting of any merit is only one which depicts the persons naturally beautiful, one which renders their physical conditions naturalistically, one which records according to the laws of perspective, the relation of the depicted persons to themselves, to the space, and in one word, one which shows the sacred scene according to any colored photograph.[23]

As a result, the same interest in "real death" that characterizes Western art has crept into Orthodox icons. Scenes that depict the agony of the Crucifixion and of martyrs became rampant over the last few centuries, during what has been called the Western captivity. Happily, in our century there is a return, in nearly all areas of the life of the Orthodox Church, to her own patristic roots. Such a renaissance is also taking place in iconography. As this movement advances, and as the icon is recognized for what it truly is, the proper understanding of death as well as of the whole of Orthodox Christian life will be reflected in her icons. The Church's vision of who she is, why she exists, and where we are going will then show itself to all "those who have eyes to see."

# NOTES

1 Constantine Kalokyris, *The Essence of Orthodox Iconography*, Brookline, Holy Cross School of Theology, Hellenic College, 1971, p. 15.

2 *Ibid.*, p. 24.

3 Leonid Ouspensky, *The Theology of the Icon*, Crestwood, St. Vladimir's, 1978, pp. 84-85.

4 *Ibid.*, p. 83.

5 *Ibid.*, pp. 95-96.

6 John Taylor, *Icon Paintings*, New York, Mayflower Books, 1979, p. 54.

7 *Ibid.*

8 Paul Evdokimov, *The Art of the Icon: A Theology of Beauty*, Redondo Beach, Calif., Oakwood, 1990, p. 280.

9 *Ibid.*, p. 279.

10 Leonid Ouspensky and Vladimir Lossky, *The Meaning of Icons*, Boston, St. Vladimir's, 1982, p. 190.

11 Evdokimov, pp. 296-297.

12 Ouspensky and Lossky, p. 114.

13 Evdokimov, p. 140.

14 *Ibid.*, pp. 314-315.

15 André Grabar, *Byzantine Painting*, New York, Rizzoli, 1979, p. 166 and p. 120.

16 Evdokimov, p. 314.

17 Ouspensky, pp. 21-38.

18 Philippe Ariès, *The Hour of Our Death*, New York, Knopf, 1981, pp. 97-98.

19 *Ibid.*, p. 98.

20 *Ibid.*, pp. 132-133.

21 Evdokimov, pp. 73-74.

22 Archimandrite Vasileios, *Hymn of Entry*, Crestwood, St. Vladimir's, 1984, pp. 89-90.

23 Kalokyris, p. 9.

# ALLEGORICAL PERSONIFICATION IN ORTHODOX ICONOGRAPHY

## INTRODUCTION

The purpose of this study is to investigate the role of personification within the artistic tradition of the Orthodox Church, that is, in icons. Since we are in the midst of a renaissance of icon painting and study, we assume that most people have a vague idea about what an icon is. The other term in the title of this study, allegorical personification, may be less familiar. By it we mean the following: the visual representation in human form of an idea, quality, or sentiment, such as wealth, sometimes an image can stand for an object or place, such as a particular city. Personification is a sub-category of allegory in that it restricts itself to human figures, but allegory in a larger sense allows for non-human figural representation as well, an example being the Soviet bear. The essential element in allegory and its sub-category personification is that the artistic forms, human or animal, are not intended to represent actual historical human persons or real animals. These images, called *signifiants*, are intended rather to point away from themselves to the abstractions, called *signifiés*, which it is difficult or impossible to represent directly. It would be an error, therefore, and a confusion of categories, to ask "Who is that person?" when dealing with an allegorical personification. The proper question to be asked is rather "What does this human form stand for?" Not to be able to distinguish between these two different kinds of human representations, not to know which category of images we are dealing with, is one of the problems of interpreting early Christian art, such as that found in the catacombs.

## THE PAGAN BACKGROUND

We know that allegory was an important element in the Græco-Roman artistic tradition: examples of such figures as the Three Graces[1] (fig. 42), Springtime[2] (fig. 43), Roman provinces[3] (fig. 44) etc. abound. We know also that the orant figure and the Good Shepherd have their roots in pagan imagery as personifications of piety and philanthropy respectively.[4] (figs 45 a-d) These forms were eventually given a Christian interpretation, but their pagan artistic ancestry goes back to allegorical personification.

Græco-Roman art included, of course, images of real historical persons as well as of mythological or heroic persons and gods. This category of representations is shared with the Christian as well as many other traditions and does not pose any special problem.

## THE CHRISTIAN BACKGROUND

Christianity entered the Græco-Roman world proclaiming that the God of Israel had intervened in history for the salvation of man. The Lord Jesus spoke and acted in front of witnesses, and the apostles proclaimed an historical Gospel whose truth rested on the fact that they had seen and heard the Holy One of Israel who was crucified under Pontius Pilate. Several New Testament passages contrast Gospel "truth" and "true religion" with myths, fables, old wives tales, and pointless speculation. (1 Tim 1:4, 4:7, 6:20; 2 Tim 2:15-16 and 4:4-5;

*Fig. 42 The Three Graces*

*Fig. 43 Springtime*

*Fig. 44 Roman Provinces*

*Fig. 45a. Pagan orant figure*

*Fig. 45b  Orant mural*

*Fig. 45c The Good Shepherd*

*Fig. 45d The Good Shepherd*

Tit 1:14) St. Peter especially contrasts "cleverly invented myths" with "the knowledge of the power and the coming of our Lord Jesus Christ" which he witnessed on the holy mountain of the Transfiguration. (2 Pet 1:16-18) When the apostles speak about Jewish genealogies, gnostic myths, or pointless philosophical speculations, they always contrast them with the historical Gospel of Christ: "the Word became flesh and dwelt among us . . . and we beheld His glory." This radical, historical orientation of the Gospel, along with a Jewish penchant for concreteness, did not leave much room for allegorical personification of abstract ideas or qualities.

Christian preachers, however, soon found themselves in a world that accorded importance to allegorical representations. The stage was thus set for a confrontation, not necessarily violent, between two different ways of representing human persons. At the beginning of Christian imagery, for example in the catacombs, we see both currents mingled together so that it is sometimes difficult to determine whether a feminine orant figure represents a real martyr, the Church, piety, all of these, or something else. Other scenes are obviously historical representations, such as illustrations of Daniel, Lazarus, and Jonah. As Christian art developed throughout the first centuries, we see a marked preference and predominance of the depiction of real people and real historical events as opposed to allegorical personification.

This historical orientation and preference was most clearly expressed in the eighty-second canon of the Council in Trullo (692):

> In some pictures of the venerable icons, a lamb is painted to which the Precursor points his finger, which is received as a type of grace, indicating beforehand through the Law, our true Lamb, Christ our God. Embracing therefore the ancient types and shadows as symbols of the truth, and patterns

given to the Church, we prefer "grace and truth," receiving it as the fulfillment of the Law. In order therefore that "that which is perfect" may be delineated to the eyes of all, at least in colored expression, we decree that the figure in human form of the Lamb who taketh away the sin of the world, Christ our God, be hence forth exhibited in images, instead of the ancient lamb, so that all may understand by means of it the depths of the humiliation of the Word of God, and that we may recall to our memory his conversation in the flesh, his passion and salutary death, and his redemption which was wrought for the whole world.[5]

Although the immediate target of the canon is not pagan allegorical personification but rather Old Testament types of the Messiah, such as a lamb, the Fathers state clearly that they "prefer" the direct image of the real historical Messiah, Jesus Christ, to indirect images of "types and shadows" which represented the Messiah before His coming. We have a definite devalorization, but not a rejection, of indirect symbols of persons when it is possible to have their direct portrait images. Although the canon deals only with Christ and his Old Testament types, its intent could also apply to Mary and any other saints symbolically prefigured in the Old Testament. Their iconic images are to be preferred to indirect symbols.

But does canon eighty-two have a bearing on allegorical personification? Not in a direct sense. We can say, however, that the affirmation of images of historical persons as opposed to a certain type of indirect symbolism shows how the Church conceives the relationship of icons to all indirect representations. The pagan artistic convention of personification is therefore indirectly devalued in the face of representations of historical scenes and persons.

We can see this preference gradually taking over in the first centuries of Christian art. The first attempts by

Christians at visual art were probably image-signs, such as the fish or anchor in the case of non-human signs, although we cannot exclude the possibility that Christ and New Testament saints were also drawn. The non-human signs either receded in importance, or were replaced by images with an increasingly historical content. This happened with the orant figure.[6] It was at first a pagan personification of the virtue of piety that had been associated with a deceased person; later it may have represented the Church; then particular saints, eventually the Mother of God, were represented as orants. The pagan *criophoros*, a man carrying a sheep on his shoulders, underwent a similar development. At first, it was a pagan symbol for the virtue of philanthropy, but in a Christian context, it became an obvious symbol for Christ the Good Shepherd. This figure may even have been used for direct representation of Christ, as in the mid-fifth century Mausoleum of Galla Placidia, where a *criophoros* is shown with halo and cross, surrounded by sheep.[7] We also notice that during the iconoclastic controversy, the defenders of icons often stated the kinds of icons to be painted, that is, what the content of icons should be. The Council of Constantinople 869–70, in its third canon states that "if anyone does not venerate the icon of Christ the Saviour, let such a one not see His face at the Second Coming. In the same way, we venerate and honor the icons of His all pure Mother, of the holy angels painted as they are described in the Holy Scriptures, and those of the saints."[8] The radically historical orientation of Christianity in general and its iconography in particular, therefore, seems well established.

## THE PROBLEM

The question we want to deal with and the problem it

raises are the following: Is there a place for the ancient symbolic form of allegorical personification in the iconography of the Orthodox Church? The thesis that we will try to defend here is that personification is a minor adjunct to the dominant historical orientation of iconography, but at various times and places, the iconographic tradition has deviated from its canonical roots by allowing allegorical personification to have an equal footing with, and sometimes to overshadow, the historical orientation. As a minor element, both in importance and in the amount of space occupied in any particular icon, personification is acceptable, though not necessary. When its size and importance grow beyond its proper place, personification then becomes a threat to the canonical tradition's theological and artistic balance.

We need to clarify one aspect of the problem, its relation to "symbolism." The word "symbol" is very elastic. When we enlarge the definition of "symbol" to include artistic images as well as verbal and mental representations, we enter the vast field of semeiology[9], that is, the science of signs and symbols. St. John of Damascus was already aware of at least seven kinds of images, both verbal and visual.[10] The scope of our study is much narrower, however, since we are dealing with a very restricted form of symbolism: a meaning, *signifié*, represented by a human form, *signifiant*, that is not a real person.

We have no objection to real historical persons being portrayed as embodiments of virtues, qualities, sins, or ideas that have been associated with them during their lives. To be likened to Quisling or to Benedict Arnold (for Americans; Canadians see him differently) conveys immediate meaning. Allegorical personification, however, is not this sort of symbolization of an historical person. It is not the adding of a meaning onto a real person but rather the visualization of an abstract meaning in a non-historical human form. Personification is the opposite of symbolic embodiment. Instead of starting with an historical person and moving to an additional meaning, personification starts with an abstraction and moves to its visualization in an empty human form. Our study deals with this second relation of meaning and human form when it expands its role to rival or overshadow the historical principle.

## THE CANONICAL TRADITION

Let us now look at some of the icons that contain personification in a proper relation to the historical principle.

### *The Epiphany Icon*

In the icon of the Baptism of Christ, we often see two human figures at Christ's feet, one a man and the other a woman; sometimes they are riding on the back of fish or sea monsters. The two figures (Fig. 46) represent the psalm verse, "The sea looked and fled, Jordan turned back." (Ps 114:3) The woman is the sea, representing the crossing of the Red Sea by Moses and the children of Israel. As such, she is a prefiguration of baptism. The man has his back to Christ and is an allegory of the Jordan. Elisha turned back the Jordan with Elijah's mantle forming a dry path through the waters; this is another prefiguration of Christian baptism.

These figures are usually small in comparison to the whole composition and represent important, but secondary, Old Testament prefigurative elements. Were they to be left out or obscured in some way, the Epiphany icon would not suffer in any essential way, and they in fact are

*Fig. 46  Epiphany, detail of figures at the feet of Christ.*

*Fig. 47 The Pentecost Icon*

not always present in these icons. It is nonetheless interesting to see how each iconographer represents these curious figures as well as the fish and sea monsters that often accompany them.

## The Pentecost Icon

In the icon of the Descent of the Holy Spirit, we have the personification of the world by a crowned man called Cosmos. He represents the world in darkness, on which, through the Church the fire of the Holy Spirit has descended. It just may be that the personification Cosmos represents a movement opposite to what we saw with the pagan orant and criophoros figures: instead of personification giving way to real people, we have the representation of real people giving way to personification. In some ancient manuscripts from around the year 1000, several people are represented in the dark space at the bottom of the icon.[11] (fig. 47), These manuscript illuminations may indicate an older and original tradition of representing real, though unnamed, persons who in turn represent all people. In that case, we would then certainly have an example of reverse development: an allegorical personification replacing real persons.

Whatever the actual historical development of the Pentecost icon may have been, we have an allegory in the figure of Cosmos who occupies the lower dark space in the composition. Although his size may limit his importance in the composition, Cosmos is by no means an unimportant figure for the icon, and his absence would alter significantly the meaning of the icon. He is necessary to complete the downward movement of the tongues of fire from God, onto the apostles, and through them onto the world sitting in darkness. The Pentecost icon therefore is perhaps the upper limit of the use of personification in the iconographic tradition, and if the manuscript tradition showing multiple uncrowned figures is an indication of an older iconographic tradition, we may even say that in Cosmos, personification has taken on an exaggerated role.

## The Hospitality of Abraham

Is this icon an example of personification? We do not think so because it is based on the story of the visit of three visitors to Abraham and Sarah; the biblical and ecclesiastical tradition considers the story to be historical, involving real people. Whether the mysterious visitors in the icon are interpreted as a trinitarian epiphany or as an appearance of the Word and two angels or men, we are still dealing with an historical event onto which a trinitarian or christological interpretation has been added. Both interpretations are in fact present in the tradition, and the biblical account itself is inconsistent in that it refers to the visitors sometimes as men and angels.[12] (Gen 18-19)

The most famous rendering of this icon is of course that of Rublev, who reduced the historical elements to a minimum and even eliminated Abraham and Sarah completely. The reduction of the historical elements naturally increases the non-temporal and non-spatial feeling surrounding the angels, but they are in fact images of actual visitors, of whatever nature, whom the tradition has interpreted in various ways. This icon is therefore not an example of allegorical personification but rather the interpretation of an historical event.

## An Image of the Adoration of the Magi

At the Dokheiariou monastery, there is a seventeenth-century fresco that resembles the Adoration of the Magi.[13] (fig. 48) It is in fact an illustration of one of the stichera sung at Christmas vespers: "What shall we offer Thee, O Christ. . . ." The Mother of God, holding the Christ Child, is placed in the middle of the image surrounded by the various elements mentioned in the sticheron. The iconographer wanted to represent each of the gifts mentioned in the text and obviously took the Christmas icon as his model. A star shines in the sky; the angels sing; the shepherds show their amazement; the Magi offer their gifts. But to represent the earth and the desert, the artist painted two women who personify these natural elements. The woman representing the earth carries a cave, and the woman represnting the desert, who looks like St. Mary of Egypt, holds a manger.

First of all, we must note that this image does not represent an event, in the strictest sense, even though elements of the Christmas icon are incorporated in it. It is rather an illustration of a liturgical text. We see that the artist has already given in to the current of his time by moving away from a strict historicity. He has given a visual form to a poetic text, and to accomplish his objective, he has combined historical elements with allegorical personification. In itself, this image does not give an exaggerated place to personification, but we know that the inspiration behind the work, that is, the desire to illustrate a text, gives artists a much greater chance to exercise their imagination, even their fantasy. This is precisely what the Church has always fought. This tendency went hand in hand with the degradation of the canonical tradition itself, and, in our opinion, this was no accident. When we see images of the Mother of God and Child seated on/in a spouting fountain (*fig. 49*), an image meant to illustrate the poetic image of "The Mother of God, the Fountain of All Joy," we need to ask ourselves if we have not descended to the level of the absurd.

*Fig. 48 17th century fresco illustrating "What shall we offer you" Docheiariou Monastery.*

*Fig. 49 The Mother of God, the Fountain of All Joy*

## Icons of Saints

Because of the wide variety among icons of the saints, it is difficult to make a survey of all such icons and to determine the place of personification in them. The very fact that images of saints are of historical persons, however, tips the balance away from an important role for this kind of symbolism. It is not to be excluded, but our guess is that it is rather rare.

We might mention, nonetheless, the four symbols for the evangelists, one of which is a winged human figure standing for St. Matthew. Is this really an image of an angel coming, from Ezekiel's vision (Ezek 1:14-25) and reflected in Revelation 4:6-8, or some other heavenly creature? Whatever may be the history and interpretation of these symbols, it is certain that the winged man is not a direct image or icon of St. Matthew. It is rather a human form symbolizing the evangelist or his gospel. Used in this context, it is a personification, but due to its Old and New Testament roots as well as its relatively infrequent usage, we cannot consider it to be an abuse of the historical principle.

Are icons of Saint Sophia and her three daughters, Faith, Hope, and Charity, meant to represent real women saints? Even if they are so intended, has Christian history simply assumed that real people stand behind what were originally allegorical personifications of Christian virtues? If this is the case, we have a very good example of how the Church feels somewhat uncomfortable with "hollow" representations of the human form. Even where there were no real saints behind the images, the Church "created" four new ones to fill the void.

## DEFORMATIONS

We have seen that the phenomenon of allegorical personification has a very minor place in the canonical tradition of iconography. There are, however, examples of what we would call real distortions in which personification takes on an exaggerated role and thus deforms the canonical tradition.

### Psalter Illustrations

Throughout the history of Christian art, there have been revivals of classical elements. Manuscript illumination is one of the art forms that has shown itself rather susceptible to the ebb and flow of these revivals. Because these images are not intended for liturgical use in the churches, though they are closely related to the icons painted in the churches, we see a greater degree of latitude and thus a lessening of the canonical requirements. A good example of the greater latitude found in illuminations is seen in the fact that the iconoclastic struggle is reflected visually in Psalter illuminations just after the iconoclastic controversy of 725–843, but is never shown in the iconography of the churches.[14]

We have an illuminated Byzantine Psalter from the eleventh century (Bibliothèque Nationale, Paris) in which there is an image of King David in the company of two female figures personifying wisdom and prophecy; they inspire David, who holds a Psalter.[15] (fig. 50) By their size and the fact that there are two figures, the personification principle is at least as important as the representation of the historical David.

### God the Father

We have a strange and aberrant use of personification in direct depictions of the Trinity, and God the Father.

We are not speaking here of the Hospitality of Abraham which is an indirect image of the Trinity. Images of an old man representing God the Father are justified as making visible, certain traits expressing the idea of the first Person's fatherhood. *(fig. 51)* Realizing that the natural tendency of Orthodox Christians on seeing a human form in an icon is to ask "Who is that?", thus assuming that a real person stands behind the image, and realizing as well that an image of the Person of the Father is impossible and impious, Bogoslovsky says that the image of an old man in relation to God the Father is a scriptural visualization of the anthropomorphisms concerning God. These images are therefore personifications of the *idea* of fatherhood and are not intended to be images of God the Father himself.[16]

Not only do we have here a major clash with the ecclesial tradition which condemns any attempt to visualize or paint the Father directly, but we also have a major clash of the personification principle with the iconographic principle which sees a human form in an icon as being the representation of the real person. In this image we see a human form which has no real person behind it; the Father's image can stand behind no created image, yet it is claimed that somehow this image represents the Father. The result is that personification is raised to the same level as the iconographic principle in a very important area, the doctrine of God, and causes a serious imbalance resulting in iconographic heresy. An allegorical personification of the idea of fatherhood is set beside an image of Christ to which is added an indirect symbolic representation of the Holy Spirit. This representation is taken out of its natural setting, that of the Baptism of Christ. Of all the other historical

*Fig. 50  11th century Byzantine Psalter showing King David with wisdom and prophecy*

and theological objections that can be made against these images of the Trinity, the one based on the improper and exaggerated use of personification is not the least among them.

We have a second use of personification to justify images of God the Father in the sophiology of Fr. Sergius Bulgakov, a Russian emigré priest who taught at St. Sergius Orthodox Institute in Paris just after the Revolution. His sophiology assumes that there is an eternal and divine humanity in God, which he calls the divine Wisdom (Sophia), and that the image of an old man is an image of God's eternal and divine humanity.[17] Bulgakov rejects the apophaticism of the Fathers, and consequently the iconology worked out at the time of the iconoclastic controversy. Such a theology believes in a God Who, essentially invisible, becomes visible in the Incarnation. Bulgakov rather claims that God is visible and representable in "his divine and eternal humanity" (divine Wisdom), which has been drawn and projected in created humanity. Leaving aside the highly questionable nature of his sophiology, the Church's iconology, as opposed to Fr. Bulgakov's, says that icons represent real persons in representable natures. Unless we want to say that the divine Wisdom is a Fourth Person of the Trinity, and Fr. Bulgakov always denied that this was his doctrine, the image of an old man representing "the eternal and divine humanity of God" can only be a personification of a non-person, a thing or idea. Whatever we want to make of Fr. Bulgakov's complicated argumentation as well as of his surprising notion of an "eternal and divine humanity – the Divine Sophia – in God," his ideas do not make the image of an old man in a direct depiction of the Trinity any more acceptable.

*Fig. 51 Direct depiction of the Trinity with God the Father personified as an image of an old man.*

*Fig. 52 16th-century image of Divine wisdom from Novgorod.*

## The Divine Sophia

In his book on iconography, Paul Evdokimov[18] explains and defends the image of the Divine Wisdom. In a late sixteenth-century Novgorod icon reproduced in his book, (fig. 52), we see the Divine Wisdom portrayed as a crowned angelic figure seated on a throne, with the Mother of God and John the Baptist on either side. Above the central figure, is Christ with a throne directly above His head and angels on either side of the throne. Evdokimov follows in the sophiological tradition of Fr. Bulgakov and sees in this enthroned angel an image of the Divine Wisdom: "And finally, the angel in the middle is Wisdom as the personified Source of energies and sanctification, pneuma-Spirit without the article." The other figures in the image represent the different ways in which wisdom has been explained. We are not concerned with them because they are, in fact, examples of what is a normal iconographic principle: real persons, human or angelic, are given a symbolic meaning. Christ is Christ; Mary is Mary; John the Baptist is himself; and the angels represent real angels. But then comes the fundamental iconographic question: "Who is that in the middle?" The answer is, of course, that it is a "non-person," but as Evdokimov says himself it is "the personified Source of energies and sanctification." The personified source of something is not a "someone" and therefore runs up against the ecclesial tradition which requires that a human form, occupying so central and dominant a position in an icon, represent someone, not something.

The first problem that we see with Evdokimov's explanation is not so much that a personification is at the center of an image, though that is a problem. The real difficulty is found in sophiological theology and its intricate and at times mystifying argumentation. Having designated the Divine Wisdom as a quasi-substantial though non-personal element in God himself, what other means but personification can the proponents of sophiology use to make an image of what they consider to be such an important principle. The personification of divine Wisdom seems aberrant because it shows that some Orthodox are not satisfied with painting Christ the Wisdom of God in His historical image. As a result, a symbolic image pushes the historical image out of the center and thus violates canon eighty-two of the Council of Trullo. Sophiological theology seems to exceed the bounds of the larger ecclesial tradition by identifying something that is "divine and eternal" in God which is neither persons, nature, or energies. The application of sophiological theology to iconography only compounds the excess.

The image of Divine Wisdom is, however, a very pointed example of the close relationship that exists between a theological vision and iconography. A contaminated theological vision will eventually manifest itself in contaminated iconography. Being a theological art form, iconography can and must be evaluated not only from an artistic perspective but also from a theological one. Personification as an artistic element, which if subordinated and overshadowed by the historical principle of iconography, can have a place, but when theologians and artists overstep the boundary established by the ecclesial tradition, personification then becomes a vehicle which corrupts the art of the Church and makes visible a heterodox theological vision.

# NOTES

1 Michael Grant, *The Art and Life of Pompeii and Herculaneum*, New Week Books, New York, 1979, p. 57.

2 *Les fresques de Pompéi*, Editions Atlas, Paris, 1983, p. 38.

3 T. Cornell and J. Matthews, *Atlas du monde romain*, Fernand Nathan, Paris, 1984, p. 203.

4 Paul Lebeau, *Aux origines de l'art chrétien*, Lumen Vitae, Brussels, 1987, pp. 17-51; Theodor Klauser, "Studien zur Entstehungsgeschicte der Christlichen Kunst" III, Jahrbuch für Antike und Christentum, Jahrgang 3 (1960).

5 *The Seven Ecumenical Councils*, Henry Percival, ed., Eerdmans, 1979, p. 401.

6 André Grabar, *Christian Iconography: A Study of Its Origins*, Princeton, pp. 74 ff.

7 Munemoto Yanagi et al, *Byzantium*, Chartwell, Secaucus, N. J., 1978, pp. 16-17.

8 Léonide Ouspensky, *Théologie de l'icône*, Cerf, Paris, 1980, p. 182.

9 Charles Bernard, "L'activité symbolique," *Théologie symbolique*, Téqui, Paris, 1978, pp. 9-124; Egon Sendler; "The Theories of the Image," *The Icon: Image of the Invisible*, Oakwood, Redondo Beach, CA, 1988, pp. 77-82.

10 St. John of Damascus, *On the Divine Images*, David Anderson, tr., St. Vladimir's, Crestwood, 1980, pp. 74-78.

11 See the reproductions of Pentecost icons in George Galavaris, *The Illustrations of the Liturgical Homilies of Gregory Nazianzinus*, Princeton University Press, Princeton, N. J., 1969; also Léonide Ouspensky, "Quelques considérations au sujet de l'iconographie de la Pentecôte" [Some Considerations on the Subject of the Iconography of Pentecost], *Messager de l'Exarchat du patriarcat russe* 33-34, Paris, 1960; Christopher Watler, "La Pentecôte", *L'iconographie des conciles dans la tradition byzantine*, Paris, Archives de l'Orient Chrétien #13, 1970, pp. 190-214.

12 L. Thunberg, "Early Christian Interpretations of the Three Angels in Gen. 18," *Studia Patristica*, VII ("Texte und Untersuchungen", 92), Berlin, 1966, pp. 560-70.

13 Philip Sherrard, *Athos the Holy Mountain*, Overlook Press, Woodstock, N.Y., 1982, p. 13.

14 Ouspensky, *Théologie de l'icône*, pp. 189-90; see the Chludov

Psalter, State Historical Museum, Moscow p. 150 and p. 152 in Robin Cormack, "Painting after Iconoclasm," *Iconoclasm: 9th Spring Symposium on Byzantine Studies*, Birmingham Centre for Byzantine Studies, University of Birmingham, U.K., 1977, pp. 142-163; André Grabar, *L'iconoclasme byzantin*, Paris, Flammarion, 1984, pp. 369-76.

15 This image is used as the cover for a French translation of the psalms from the Greek Septuagint. *Les psaumes: prières de l'Eglise*, Père Placide Deseille, tr., YMCA-Press, Paris, 1979.

16 See the discussion of Bogoslovsky's justification, Ouspensky, *Théologie de l'icône*, pp. 361-63.

17 See the section on Bulgakov's doctrine in Ouspensky, pp. 363-68; E. Behr-Sigel, "La sophiologie du Père S. Boulgakov," *Le messager orthodoxe* #57/ I-1972, pp. 21-48; Nicolas Ozoline, "La doctrine boulgakovienne de la 'descriptibilité' de Dieu à la lumière de la théologie orthodoxe de l'icône" [Bulgakov's Doctrine of God's "Describability" in the Light of the Orthodox Theology of the Icon], *Le messager orthodoxe* #98/I-II-1985, pp. 111-129.

18 Paul Evdokimov, "The Icon of the Divine Wisdom," *The Art of the Icon: a Theology of Beauty*, Oakwood, Redondo Beach, CA, 1990; John Meyendorff, "L'iconographie de la Sagesse divine dans la tradition byzantine" [The Iconography of the Divine Wisdom in the Byzantine Tradition], *Byzantine Hesychasm: Historical, Theological and Social Problems*, Variorum Reprints, London 1974, pp. 259-277.

# ORTHODOX ICONOGRAPHY
## & THE NON-ORTHODOX

As almost anyone who follows popular movements is aware, we are in the midst of a renaissance of Orthodox iconography. We see icons everywhere, sometimes in the strangest places. A multitude of books has been published on the subject, and many people, Orthodox and non-Orthodox, are turning their hand to icon painting. We should view this renewal of interest in iconography as a blessing because it makes possible a wider proclamation of the Orthodox faith. Icons are, in fact, the faith of the Orthodox Church made visible in an artistic medium. On the other hand, certain aspects of the contemporary renewal should trouble us and require a free and open discussion in order to formulate a reasoned and balanced evaluation. One such question is the following: How appropriate is it for non-Orthodox to paint icons?

Because icons are à la mode today, many non-Orthodox want to paint them, for a variety of reasons: the gamut runs all the way from authentically pious and well-meaning Roman Catholic and Protestant Christians to utterly unbelieving artists whose imitation of the iconic style aims only at cashing in on a lucrative market. We Orthodox Christians are obliged to adopt some attitude toward the non-Orthodox who paint icons. Their activity poses a problem because the Orthodox Church believes iconography to be hers for at least two reasons: *historical* and *theological*.

I say *historical* because the so-called iconic style has for a long time been limited to the Orthodox Churches. For many centuries, icons have played little or no part in the artistic development of the Roman Catholic or Protestant Churches. The very fact that Western Christians are learning to appreciate icons shows that, for Catholics, the tradition was lost. For Protestants, icons have never played a part in their religious awareness.

I say *theological* because from the Orthodox point of view, icons are not simply works in a particular artistic "style," be it Byzantine, Russian, or what have you. Icons have a theological content. They make visible the faith which is also expressed in the Bible, liturgy, hymns, canons, writings of the Fathers, architecture, lives of the saints, etc. If the vision of faith which stands behind icons is poorly expressed, or falsified in some way, it is altogether proper to speak of heretical or heterodox art – that is, art that falsifies or distorts God's revelation in Christ. What is important is not that the icons be beautiful since beauty lies in the eye of the beholder; the very concept changes with times and cultures. Rather, it is essential that icons faithfully make visible the vision of faith of the Church. Icons that fulfill this function are called canonical. If canonical icons are æsthetically beautiful, all the better. Who would not prefer a beautiful icon to an ugly or amateurish one? If, however, the choice is between a canonical icon of questionable æsthetic quality and a magnificent, though uncanonical painting, the answer should be obvious. I emphasize *should* because those who have studied the history of icons know very well that Orthodox Christians themselves have not always preferred canonicity to so-called beauty. We have only to visit certain Orthodox churches to see that confusion between the two still reigns.

Canonical Orthodox iconography is then essentially an ecclesial art. It is art of, by, and for the Orthodox Church and its vision of faith. This art has been developed by those who professed that faith and who consciously wanted to express and to transmit Holy Tradition. Iconographers were, and are, expected to live in spiritual communion with the Church, to be in the process of being personally transfigured by her vision, and to submit themselves to her guidance. Although historically this guidance has not always been all it should have been, the ecclesial consciousness has always existed and claims that through her iconographers, the Church paints to express her vision of faith. It is her legitimate right to supervise those who wish to offer their artistic talents to Christ and his Church.

The ecclesiastical solicitude for artists and their work has been expressed in the canons of various councils. Perhaps the first historical statement of this kind is canon 73 of the Quinisext Council in 692. After forbidding the painting of crosses on church floors where people could walk on them, the canon states, "Therefore those who from this present (time) represent on the pavement the sign of the cross, we decree are to be cut off."[1] The Council of Constantinople held in 869–870 to depose Patriarch Photius (for Roman Catholics, the Eighth Ecumenical Council; for the Orthodox, a local but orthodox council) passed the following canon 7 concerning iconographers:

> The painting of holy and precious icons, as well as teaching the precepts of divine and human wisdom, is of great usefulness. It is not good therefore that these things be done by unworthy persons. This is why, under no circumstances, do we authorize excommunicated persons to paint icons in the holy churches; for the same reason, they cannot teach until

they have turned away from their error. After this decision which we have made, if any such person attempts to paint holy icons in the church, let him be deposed if he is a cleric and deprived of the holy Mysteries if he is a layman.[2]

The Stoglav Council (Council of One-Hundred Chapters) in Moscow, 1551, in deciding the question of the proper portrayal of the Trinity made the following pronouncement in chapter 41:

> Consult the divine rules and tell us what usage should be followed. Answer: painters must paint icons according to ancient models, as Greek painters, Andrei Rublev and other well-known painters painted them. . . . Painters must not follow their own fantasies in anything.[3]

Chapter 43 continues:

> In each of their dioceses, the bishops will pay a great deal of untiring attention and care to see that good icon-painters and their students paint according to the ancient models and do not paint God according to their own ideas or suppositions. . . . The council decrees that those who presently have painted icons without having learned how, arbitrarily, without practice and without following the [standard] image . . . must be required to learn from good masters. Whoever, by the grace of God, starts to paint in the image and likeness, let him paint. Whoever God has deprived of this gift, let him completely stop painting so that God's name will not be blasphemed by such painting. . . . Archbishops and bishops, in all the cities, villages and monasteries of their dioceses, will inspect icon-painters and personally examine their works. . . . The archbishops and bishops will personally inspect the painters that they have put in charge of inspecting others and will control them with all strictness. . . .[4]

The preceding citations from canonical sources show clearly that the Orthodox Church considers it not only proper to watch over the canonicity of icons but also to be concerned about the iconographers themselves. As far as I know, the question of non-Orthodox iconographers has never been raised historically, but we Orthodox today cannot avoid it and still remain faithful to the ecclesial consciousness of Orthodoxy that says that icons express her vision of faith and that iconographers are instruments for the transmission of that vision and tradition. Guided by their pronouncements forbidding excommunicated persons (Council of 869–870) and untalented or immoral persons (Stoglav) from painting, we can imagine without too much difficulty the Fathers' reaction to heterodox icon-painters producing icons for themselves or for Orthodox churches. Such painters represent at best an anomaly and at worst a sacrilege, depending on a series of variables such as talent, morality, canonicity, etc. How can those who do not share the Orthodox vision of faith and do not live in her sacramental communion represent and transmit that vision?

We cannot get away from the idea that icon painting is an ecclesial and theological art. The only basis on which non-Orthodox can paint icons, assuming they respect the outward elements of canonicity, is the personal basis. Protestant or Roman Catholic Christians do paint icons for their own and for others' personal, spiritual lives, but this artistic activity cannot be, from the Orthodox point of view, an ecclesial activity. While some Roman Catholics paint icons, their Church as an ecclesial entity does not paint icons. The same is true for Protestant Christians. The distinction is fundamental. It is between what an individual does as his personal expression of piety and what the Church does, through the instrument of an iconographer, to express her very nature, her vision of faith.

Icon painting is precisely not the personal activity

of artists who exercise their talents by painting scenes with a religious content. From ancient times up to the present, iconographers have been told not to let their personal imaginings and fantasies dictate the content of their works. They are rather to follow Holy Tradition. Although I concede that some non-Orthodox show a remarkably Orthodox sensitivity and can paint icons which are preferable to works painted by Orthodox, the activity of these artists can never rise above the personal level to become an ecclesial activity. These non-Orthodox artists, though we can hope that they will learn and follow as strictly as possible the outward canonical requirements, are in fact very often open to currents and influences which turn their "icons" into religious paintings in the Byzantine style. Even when good faith is assumed on the part of these Christians, they lack the stabilizing influence of Holy Tradition which can correct certain distortions. It is in fact that very Holy Tradition which has brought about the renaissance among the Orthodox and is turning the tide on decades, even centuries, of decadence. It is virtually impossible to imagine that the iconographic reawakening could have come from Catholic or Protestant initiatives.

I am fully aware that much of the bad iconography we see in our churches today was done by Orthodox painters, and being Orthodox does not in itself guarantee the ability to paint canonical icons of high quality. As much discernment is required for judging paintings done by Orthodox artists as for judging paintings done by non-Orthodox artists. Nonetheless, a common loyalty to the Orthodox vision of faith makes correction, improvement, and renewal possible. As Orthodox Christians, we must first know and understand the depths of the treasure we posses and then try to guide the non-Orthodox of good faith to see that this activity, in order to be truly authentic, must be done by Christians in full communion with Holy Orthodoxy. In the final analysis, we do them spiritual harm by saying nothing and continuing to allow them to play with spiritual fire. Let us speak the truth in love.

# NOTES

1 *The Seven Ecumenical Councils, The Nicene and Post-Nicene Fathers* 14, Eerdmans, 1979, p. 398.

2 Leonid Ouspensky, *La Théologie de l'icône*, Paris, Editions du Cerf, p. 185, note 20. The English translations are mine.

3 *Ibid.*, p. 265.

4 *Ibid.*, pp. 267, 273-274.

# Iconography and
# St. Gregory Palamas

## Introduction

 In the Orthodox Church, sacred art is not a matter of individual taste or style, but a dogmatic matter having to do with the very heart of the Christian faith. It is an expression in visible artistic forms of the dogmatic basis of the Church herself. Therefore, the Church is very concerned about how well iconography reflects her basic beliefs: she should be able to see her faith reflected in her art. If the faith is not reflected, or only poorly reflected, then we can assume that there is something wrong with the art or that false assumptions about the faith are being made.

The doctrines of St. Gregory Palamas are also dogmatic matters for the Orthodox Church; we cannot be Orthodox and reject the fourteenth century conciliar decisions on the matter of essence and energies. It follows logically, then, that this doctrine should somehow be reflected in the Church's iconography. In this study, I propose to investigate the Palamite doctrine of essence and energies along with its manifestation in Church art. I will first set out the doctrine itself and then apply it generally and specifically to icons.

## The Doctrine of
## Essence and Energies

The God who created all things is a God who in His very being, His essence, is beyond all knowledge and is transcendent to, and untouched by, any created thing. The *essence of God* means what He is in Himself, what makes Him God and not an angel, for example. In His essence, He is radically different from the created order; therefore, one of the fundamentals in theology affirms the impassable gulf between the uncreated God and the created universe.

Though we cannot know or touch God in His essence, we do believe that He touches us; He makes Himself known, knowable, and accessible to us in the created order by means of His energies. The natural energies of God are God Himself; they come from His essence but are not the essence itself. The energies are not created powers either. They radiate, however, from the essence as rays from the sun or radioactivity from uranium, thus creating, sustaining, and sanctifying all things. By these energies, God reveals Himself to us as Trinity so that the three Persons sharing the same hidden divine essence also radiate the energies. We are able, therefore, to truly know and participate in God Himself by being bathed in His energies. We become "radioactive," as it were, to the degree that we allow God to penetrate, transform, and transfigure us with His energies.

Salvation is defined as the progressive establishment, in us individually, in the Church collectively, of the new transfigured humanity of Christ. The process and the goal are called deification, the acquisition of the Holy Spirit, the establishment of the Kingdom of God. The new creation in Christ is the Kingdom which is inaugurated in the Church and will be completed on the Day of the Lord, the Eighth Day, at the end of time. This new creation is the resurrected and renewed humanity in the transfigured cosmos, the New Jerusalem spoken about in Revelation.

One of the principal forms in which the energies of God are manifested is in the uncreated Light, the Light of the Transfiguration of Christ. Since the salvation process, the transfiguring of man, is accomplished in the total man (mind, heart, spirit, emotions, body), all aspects of him are affected by deification; it is, therefore, the belief of the Church that transfigured human beings, if God wills, can see the uncreated Light. This vision is the seeing of a real, though non-material, Light; it is not simply a metaphorical, intellectual, or symbolic phenomenon. The seeing is real also because the whole man, including the physical eyes, is transfigured and transported into the New Day, into the heavenly Jerusalem, where all things are made new. The uncreated Light which shone on Mt. Tabor in Christ's Transfiguration is God manifesting Himself in His energies. As God grants, to the degree we are able to receive it, we may be caught up in this heavenly vision and so see, and manifest ourselves, the transfiguring power of God which works for the building up of the Kingdom here on earth.

## GENERAL PRINCIPLES

Before we see how this doctrine manifests itself in iconography, we must take a look at the general purpose of icons in the Church. The first thing we must get out of our minds is that icons are *simply* decorations used to beautify the Church. Secondly, they are not *simply* pedagogical helps in teaching the truths of the faith: What the Bible teaches in words, the pictures in Church teach in art. Icons do in fact serve these two purposes, but such is not their principal reason for being. The Church uses icons primarily to portray the New Creation, the transformed cosmos, the Kingdom of God come in its final fullness. Icons are not meant to portray things,

219

people, and events as they appear in the world as we know it. Our present world is one dominated by sin, corruption, and death; things happen here that are not a part of the original or the restored creation. Although there is a connection, a continuity between our present state and the new humanity of the Kingdom, the same laws and conditions are not at all operative.

Notice the difference between the so-called natural human condition of the apostles and the condition of Jesus' humanity after the Resurrection: they are similar but different. We get a glimpse of restored humanity in the scenes of interaction between the resurrected Jesus and the apostles. Icons are meant to depict the new world of the resurrection, humanity as it will be, not as it is now:

> the whole content of Orthodox iconography . . . concerns . . . the new heaven and the new earth of Christ's redemptive work, the man and the world of regeneration. It is not concerned with the "old," the "natural," the "transient." That is to say, Orthodox iconography represents the world regenerated by divine Grace, the world where the unsetting light of God dominates.[1]

The primary biblical text for the vision of the new world comes from St. John's vision in Revelation:

> Then I saw a new heaven and a new earth; the first heaven and the first earth had disappeared. . . . I saw the holy city and the new Jerusalem, coming down from God out of heaven. . . . Here God lives among men. . . . He will wipe away all tears . . . there will be no more death, and no more mourning or sadness: Now I am making the whole creation new. . . . (Rev 21:1-5, Jerusalem Bible.)

> In the spirit, he took me to the top of an enormous, high mountain and showed me Jerusalem, the holy city. . . . It had all the radiant glory of God and glittered like some jewel of crystal clear diamond. . . . (Rev 21:10-12)

> . . . and the city did not need the sun or the moon for light since it was lit by the radiant glory of God and the Lamb was

a lighted torch for it. The pagan nations will live by its light. . . . The gates of it will never be shut by day – and there will be no night there. . . . (Rev 21:23-26)

It will never be night again and they will not need lamp-light or sunlight because the Lord will be shining on them. (Rev 22:5)

The image of a non-material light emanating from God is also present in the creation story: "God said, 'Let there be light,' and there was light." Although it is not very clear what kind of light this was, created or uncreated, it is definitely not natural light coming from heavenly bodies since these were not created until the fourth day. The strange character of this light is under-lined by the distinction between "day and night" and "morning and evening." Before there were natural light sources (sun, stars, and moon), there was something called "day" which was the presence of this primordial light; there was also something called "night," its ab-sence. What is of God, then, is only light and day; darkness and night are what is left, nothingness:

> According to the biblical story of the creation, in the begin-ning "Evening came and morning came: the first day." The six-day creation story, the *hexameron*, does not know "night." Darkness and night are not created by God. For the moment, night is only a sign of non-existence, the abstract nothingness which is "separated" from being by its very na-ture. Morning and evening denote the succession of events; they designate the creative progression of things and only form "day" which is a dimension of pure light. The opposite of "day," that is "night," is not yet the effective power of darkness. According to the meaning given to it in John's gos-pel, night only appears with the fall.[2]

So what we have here in these two biblical passages is a linking of the mysterious light of the first day of crea-tion with that of the last day of the recreation. We find ourselves in the middle living by the natural light of the heavenly sources but looking forward to the day when that light will be replaced by the creating and re-creating Light of God.

It is quite easy now to move to the realm of concrete icons where we will notice that one of the basic principles of this art is that no natural light source is depicted. Such light is excluded, unnecessary; as in the New Jerusalem and at the creation, the Lord Himself, or the Lord shining in His transfigured saints, is the Light. There are no shadows painted either, as they would indicate the direction of a light source. Here is another indication of the different character of iconic light:

> Icons depicting events which took place in daytime are no brighter than those showing us events which took place at night. The Last Supper and the prayer in Gethsemane are no darker than the Lord with the Samaritan woman at Jacob's well, the Resurrection or Pentecost.[3]

Some would say that there is here only an accidental parallel of light symbolism between the special new light of the Holy City and the lack of natural light sources in icons. We maintain, however, that the divine energy manifested as uncreated Light, dogmatically defined in the fourteenth century, is the same Light spoken of in Revelation and which, in an artistic mode, illumines the icons of the Church. Since icons portray the new creation where the uncreated Light of God illumines all, they must necessarily exclude the light sources of our fallen world since they have no place in the Kingdom.

So we must understand that the idea of the presence of divine energies as Light in icons is fundamental to understanding them. The doctrine of this Light permeates all icons; it is iconography's foundational principle. Even if there were no other indication of the presence of this doctrine in icons, the understanding that they portray the Kingdom in its fullness would be enough to establish the doctrine's importance for iconography.

We must also understand that the fourteenth-century councils did not create a new doctrine: this is not the function of any dogmatic decision. Rather, they codified and gave words to what was the unexpressed and assumed faith of the Church from the beginning. The councils excluded once and for all any merely symbolic meaning of the references in Scripture and the Fathers to this Light, if we take *symbolic* to mean not real but metaphorical. Icons were painted in their present canonical manner long before the doctrinal background was set out. The Light referred to is a real manifestation of God Himself in His energies, in His transforming, renewing, and transfiguring work of redemption.

Another basic principle which underlies faithful Church art and which is related to the Palamite doctrine is the double nature of the uncreated Light. It is 1) a thing seen because we see light as it shines in darkness; it is also 2) a medium since it allows other things to be seen. Depending on many physical factors such as quality, intensity, color, source, type, etc., the objects we see will appear different under varying light conditions. Different kinds of light can actually determine the nature of the objects seen in that light. We find the same effect on the level of the uncreated Light. Since we believe that salvation is the transformation of the whole person into the deified humanity of Christ, all our senses, among them our sight, are affected. So, as we are more and more transfigured, our sight will also be transformed so that we can see not only the Light of Tabor, if God so wills, but also ordinary things in a different Light. What, to ordinary and untransfigured eyes, may be a human derelict, will be, to transfigured eyes, an icon of God as much in need of restoration as the viewer himself.

Paul Evdokimov summarizes the point this way:

> The Taboric light is not only the object of the vision, but it is also its condition: "Whoever participates in the divine energies . . . in a sense becomes light himself. He is united to light, and with the light, he sees what remains hidden to those who do not have this grace. He thus goes beyond the physical senses and everything that is known [by the human mind]. . . ."[4]

The implication for contemplating icons is clear. For those who have untransfigured, "natural" eyes, who do not have eyes to see, icons will have little meaning. Such persons will see a picture about a religious subject that may look like a poorly drawn cartoon. Even more sophisticated eyes, the artistically trained eyes of an art critic, for example, not filled with the transforming Light of Christ, will see only an example of Byzantine or Russian religious art of a particular era manifesting certain stylistic characteristics, etc., etc. Such a critic will see all the exterior aspects, and not really see at all; he will miss the inner meaning completely. In fact, he may even be quite talented in technically reproducing icons for sale, but at the same time be an unbeliever. For those who have eyes to see, an icon is a window on eternity, a locus of communion with the transfigured persons depicted. As the persons themselves radiated the divine energies when alive on earth, and as do their relics now, so their icons are also points of radiation whereby we can have communion with them. Both media and objects, the divine energies have transformed a material painting into a vision that transcends the earthly, unre-created cosmos, transporting us into the New Heaven and the New Earth. So, again, the doctrine defined in the fourteenth century is quite relevant to the definition of what an icon does, as well as of what it shows. Without Palamite theology standing behind Church art, our understanding of icons and their use would not be so clear or complete.

## SPECIFICS

Let us now turn to actual icons to see by what means the doctrine of essence-energies is depicted. We will be dealing only with the energies as uncreated Light since, according to the doctrine, the divine essence is unknown, indescribable and, therefore, unpaintable. However, I have heard a different interpretation which I mention as the belief of one iconographer relating to the essence-energies doctrine in icons: the gold background of icons represents the essence, and the gold that is seen on actual figures in the icons represents the energies shining through. I have not been able to confirm this idea in any sources.

Paul Evdokimov, however, gives another interpretation:

> Even in technical terms, the icon's golden background is called "light" and the artistic method is called "progressive enlightenment." At the beginning of his work, the iconographer covers the face with a dark color. Then he puts on a brighter color obtained by adding some yellow ochre to the previous mixture. In effect, he adds light. This procedure of adding brighter and brighter colors on top of each other is repeated many times. Thus the progressive appearance of a human face on the icons follows a parallel progression which produces in living persons an increase of light, a greater degree of transfiguration.[5]

Evdokimov also says that since the energies are visible icons of the invisible essence, we can treat any representation of the energies as an iconic depiction of the essence.[6] As the Son is the visible image of the invisible Father so an icon of the Son is an icon of the Father, though not a direct depiction of the Father, an impossible thing; what we have is an icon of an icon.

The icon of the Transfiguration has a special place in Orthodox art and theology. It is the depiction of this event which the Orthodox use as an image of the transfiguring process itself. Since on this icon we see Christ bathed, shining in the uncreated Light, the breaking forth of the light and energies of the age to come, we need to study it carefully.

Its importance is shown by its use in the initiation of an iconographer into his art. His eyes must be transfigured to see the transfigured world; the iconographer can then paint the transfiguration, an image of the world to come:

> In former times, every iconographer-monk began his "divine art" by painting the icon of the Transfiguration. This living and direct initiation taught him, above all, that the icon is painted not so much with colors as with the Taboric light.[7]

On the icon of the Transfiguration, we see Christ on the mountain in the center of a group of circles of blue-white light, called a mandorla; sometimes other colors are used. This mandorla is also seen in the icons of the Dormition, the Ascension, and the Descent into Hell. Not all icons of Christ, however, have mandorlas; they usually appear only when some spectacular breakthrough of the divine Light is represented. The mandorla is the iconic representation of the uncreated Light. On the Transfiguration icon, the uncreated Light is shining on the three disciples. In some icons, rays are shown descending onto them, emphasizing that they beheld the Light individually. The troparion of this feast states that the disciples "beheld the Light as far as they were able to see it," thus indicating the various levels of their spiritual progress. Sometimes there is a star superimposed on the mandorla which represents the luminous cloud, another symbol of the Light; this cloud descended on the mountain and on Christ and is a sign of the Holy Spirit.

In the icon of Theophany, a ray is shown coming down from a partial circle at the top of the icon, usually with a dove in the middle of the ray, representing the Holy Spirit. The single ray then breaks into three and descends on Christ. We often see this partial circle in icons of a less spectacular divine manifestation. The same design is seen in the Nativity icon, but with a star in the place of the dove. In the following text by Evdokimov, we have the only written reference I have found to confirm, at least partially, the oral testimony referred to above concerning the representability of the divine essence:

> The Christmas and Epiphany icons show the same three-rayed light; on the Epiphany icon, this indicates the ethereal presence of the dove, a presence that is guessed at rather than seen. In the Christmas icon, the star of Bethlehem shines out of the sacred triangle inscribed in the divine sphere. . . . A single ray comes out of the upper triangle and signifies the one essence of God, but as it comes out of the star, the ray divides into three so as to indicate the participation of the three persons in the economy of salvation.[8]

Ouspensky offers a different, vaguer opinion:

> In accordance with the gospel text cited above, in the upper part of the icon, there is a segment of a circle symbolizing the open heavens. . . . This segment of a circle signifies the presence of God which sometimes is emphasized still more by a hand, blessing. Thence are shed upon the Saviour rays of light.[9]

> This ray connects the star with part of the sphere which goes beyond the limits of the icon – a symbolic representation of the heavenly world.[10]

If the circle represents the presence of God, then it is certain that it represents the energies because God is only present in this world in His energies and not in His essence.

For dogmatic reasons, I tend to agree with Ouspensky and Lossky and not to identify the partial circle with the essence, which is uncircumscribable and unknowable. Even though the circle is appropriately black, symbolizing the divine darkness, black has still another meaning in icons: death, sin, nothingness. Such a two-fold definition of darkness fits in quite well, however, with the opinion of Pseudo-Dionysius the Areopagite, who spoke about two darknesses. For Dionysius, there is on the one hand the darkness symbolizing absolute nothingness out of which we were created and toward which we slip as we sin and die and, on the other hand, the super-essential darkness above all light, where God dwells in His unknowable essence. In fact, this second "darkness" is really the result of an overabundance of light, like that causing St. Paul's blindness on the road to Damascus. It is also appropriate that the two darknesses, one due to a lack of light and the other due to too much light, are found at the top and bottom sections of icons. The upper one is the circle representing the divine darkness, and the lower one in holes, caves, and dark rivers, is the absolute nothingness. In between the two is the created world ever moving away from absolute nothingness toward the full being of the super-essential darkness. Such an interpretation, at least, fits the iconographic layout, but the dogma of the Church, as opposed to Dionysius' opinions, seems to speak against any direct iconic representations of the unknown essence.

Other ways of representing the divine energies are seen on the icon of Pentecost, the Descent of the Holy

Spirit: here the tongues of fire form the half-circle. Perhaps the tongues are right on the heads of each apostle to indicate, as the doctrine states, that although there is only one "kind" of energy, so to speak, it is distributed and multiplied for the sustaining and perfecting of the creation. As "there is one Spirit but many gifts," so there is one energy causing multiple effects in the creation; that is why "energy" is often used in the plural.

We can take notice of a phenomenon in many icons which shows people and objects giving off a glow as though they are illuminated from inside; according to the doctrine, of course, they do radiate the energies from inside. Since there is no natural light source to cause reflections and shadows, the light must come from within. The rocks and iconic mountains also appear to glow; people's clothing shows signs of being on fire, radioactive. Such phenomena indicate that all of nature (man, rocks, plants, everything) is to be transfigured in the uncreated Light.

A word needs to be said about halos. Since there are only two dimensions in icons, halos appear as circles around the heads of saints, but in fact they represent spheres since the Light shines forth from the person's whole body. Halos are not simply flat plates set on top of the saints' heads as is sometimes shown in Western religious art. Such halos are signs of holiness but not necessarily connected with any doctrine of an uncreated Light: "The halos which encircle the heads of the saints on their icons are not simply distinctive signs of their holiness but the shining forth of their bodies' luminosity."[11] Orthodox halos are always circular, not oval which would indicate a third dimensional plane. Three dimensions, except in bas-relief, are rare; they are too intimately tied to our own world. It is more difficult for three dimensions than for two to depict the transcendence of this world and to manifest the mystery of the Kingdom.

There does not seem to be any consistent practice in regards to halos; sometimes they are not present when we would expect them. This lack of consistency is especially present in reference to Old Testament figures. It is interesting to note that Adam and Eve rarely have halos in the icon of the Descent into Hell. Why, on one side of this same icon, do David and Solomon have halos and not Moses on the other? There are cases of non-saints, such as emperors and donors to specific churches, who are given halos. Some persons, living at the time of the paintings, have even been shown with square halos to distinguish them from dead saints.[12]

Duplication and triplication of symbols also exist: some saints and especially Christ are shown with individual halos within a mandorla; there may also be a halo and a star within the mandorla. In the Pentecost icon, halos are sometimes combined with the tongues of fire; rays from the half-circle can also go with halos. As stated above, there does not seem to be any clear-cut system for deciding who should get a halo or with what other symbols it can be combined.

## CONCLUSION

We have seen that there are both general principles and specific techniques which set forth the Church's dogmatic belief about the uncreated energies and the unknowable essence of God. Throughout the history of the Church, various ages have more or less adequately expressed this belief in art, and we know that in certain periods the dogmatic vision was practically lost. The Church's art became a servile imitation of Western art using foreign models, techniques, and theory. Though the vision of the uncreated Light was dimmed during these long years, the joyous renaissance of proper Orthodox theology and its expression in canonical iconography in our time shows that the vision, though darkened and dimmed, was not extinguished.

# NOTES

1 Kalokyris, Constantine, *The Essence of Orthodox Iconography*, Brookline, Mass., Holy Cross School of Theology, Hellenic College, 1971, p. 24.

2 Evdokimov, Paul, *The Art of the Icon: A Theology of Beauty*, Redondo Beach, Calif., Oakwood, 1990, pp. 5-6.

3 Vasileios, Archm., *Hymn of Entry*, Crestwood, NY, St. Vladimir's, 1984, pp. 85-86.

4 Evdokimov, p. 233, quoting St. Gregory Palamas, "Homily on the Presentation of the Holy Virgin in the Temple," *Sem. Kond.* VII, p. 138.

5 *Ibid.*, pp. 186-187.

6 *Ibid.*, p. 234.

7 *Ibid.*, p. 299.

8 *Ibid.*, p. 237.

9 Leonid Ouspensky and Vladimir Lossky, *The Meaning of Icons*, Crestwood, NY, St. Vladimir's, 1982, p. 164.

10 *Ibid.*, p. 159.

11 Evdokimov, pp. 187-188.

12 André Grabar, *Byzantine Painting*, New York, Rizzoli, 1979, pp. 50-51 and pp. 78-79.

# "Man as the Image of God" in St. Gregory of Nyssa & in Orthodox Iconography

## Introduction

Christ is the new Adam, and we are made part of a new humanity in Him even though this new humanity is not really new. It is the old humanity restored to what it was in the beginning, to what God had intended it to be all along. Christ restored the image of God in man to its purity, a purity that Adam and Eve had lost. We learn about this original state of man in the image of God from the story of creation in Genesis, which is one of the fundamental sources of Christian anthropology. This image of God in man, pure and totally renewed in Christ, is only partially restored in us and will not attain its fulfillment until all things are restored in Christ in the Kingdom. In other words, we are in the interim period between the original fall that corrupted the image of God in us and its complete restoration. We know quite well what our condition is now, but it is "only through a glass darkly" that we know what it was in paradise and what it will be in the Kingdom. Here, though, are the important questions: What parts of our present condition were in the original package, and what parts will enter the Kingdom? What really appertains to the image of God in man, to his real nature, and what part is due to the fall? By what method does/will the restoration take place? These questions have to do with the nature of man himself. Everyone agrees that there are aspects of man's present condition which we do not like and would like to change, but one of the fundamental problems in general, and specifically for this study, is how man as the image of God is to be restored. Is he to be reestablished by "surgery" or by healing: by removing something added on by the fall, or by reordering elements disordered by the fall? The method of achieving this goal will be different in each case: as different as tumor surgery is from a treatment to reestablish a diabetic's sugar and insulin balance.

The question of the destruction of something in man as he is now or the reordering of his present make-up for entrance into the Kingdom is important because St. Gregory of Nyssa had very definite ideas as to what the nature of the image of God in man is, was, and will be. He also prescribed what should be done to move ahead into the Kingdom. And his ideas have had no small influence in Church history. This issue is important for iconography also because icons portray, not the present, fallen world, but the new restored world of the Kingdom where, as far as human beings are concerned, the image of God in us will shine so brilliantly that no natural light will be needed because we and the whole creation will be transparent to and carriers of the divine Light.

Canonical Orthodox iconography is a vehicle for the Church's teaching. By studying icons, we should be able to get some insights into this question that will help us to critique St. Gregory's ideas. Here then is the format of this study: to examine St. Gregory's anthropology, his views on man as the image of God; to see what iconography has to say and show on the matter; and finally to critique St. Gregory's position in the light of iconography.

## St. Gregory's Doctrine of Man

According to St. Gregory, man was created in a two-step process; man and Adam are not exactly the same thing. There were two creations: the first took place outside time and space and relates only to mankind in general and in its undifferentiated totality. Genesis 1:26-27 says, "Let us make man in our own image, after our likeness. . . . So God created man in His own image, in the image of God He created him. . . ." As the reflection of the uncreated God within the created order, man possessed in the form of virtues all the qualities of God but refracted them through the prism of the created order: immortality, goodness, immateriality, rationality, dominion, etc. There were no imperfections in man at all. This first, ideal, and perfect creation of man in the image of God reflects St. Gregory's Platonism in that he saw the truest, the "really real" reality in non-material, spiritual, and rational terms. Since God is supremely non-material, etc., man must be also. So St. Gregory kept the basic Platonic distinction between the ideal and material worlds by postulating a first, spiritual creation of man in God's image.

God's second creation is of Adam and Eve in time and space as material, sexual, and mortal. In the first creation, man was without sexual distinction, not even bisexual, but in the second creation the original unity was broken, and the nature of man is displayed in polar sexual opposites. St. Gregory bases his idea of a second creation on a separation of the first half of Gn 1:27, quoted above, from the second half: "male and female he created them." He also based his interpretation on an existing tradition running back through Origen at least to Philo the Jew in Alexandria. There is nothing in the biblical text, however, to suggest this idea, but because the text speaks first of man and then of male and female, the verse serves as a convenient vehicle for St. Gregory's pre-existing philosophical point of view. Since this second creation was on the material level, its reality is thereby diminished; therefore, the elements pertaining to it are not part of the image of God in man as made in the first creation. These aspects of man's being (materiality, irrationality, sexuality, mortality, etc.) were given to men and women because God foresaw that His creature made in His image and likeness – St. Gregory does not follow the patristic tradition of distinguishing these two – would not use his free will to love his creator but would turn to himself as the source of his being and thus whither. Being a fallen creature, man received those things which made him like the animals so that, rather than become extinct through death, Adam and Eve were able to reproduce themselves by sexual means even though their offspring would also be mortal and fallen. When man, the purely spiritual image of God, was mixed with the purely material, i.e., a body, sensual life was given to it, and the composite being of body, soul, and spirit appeared. Thus human beings as we know them came to be. Though the material and sensual aspects of man were not part of the original image, historical men and women were to show forth the spiritual image of God in them through the instrument of their material bodies by dominating them and the rest of creation – mind over matter – until the fullness of God's purpose could be worked out in history.

These material and sensual parts, although not part of the original image, were necessary in the fallen world. By falling into materiality, human beings acquired what St. Gregory called "garments of skin," (Gen 3:21), that grossly animal life which relates us to the animals. These garments of skin are accretions and basically foreign to us; they are "sexual intercourse, conception, parturition, impurities, suckling, feeding, evacuation, gradual growth to full size, prime of life, old age, disease, and death."[1] Though these aspects of animal life are not evil in themselves since they are natural and proper for animals, they are alien but necessary elements for men and women in history. They nonetheless introduce irrational and passionate forces into human life, which, if not controlled by the higher, rational faculty, namely the image of God, can absorb the attention of the rational spirit, drag it still further from God, and orient man's whole being toward "gross animality." If, however, each person orients his being toward God by ascetical and spiritual efforts in the Church, he can use and purify the passions for good by turning them into virtues. But since they, like other features of animality assumed as the garments of skin, will be shed in death, men will move toward the restoration of the immaterial image which will no longer be affected or influenced by the passions.

Such an anthropology was difficult to square with one of the major Christian doctrines, the Resurrection. Platonism does not envision the restoration of any material or bodily life after death, yet because he was a Christian, St. Gregory had to work that belief into his system. This was not easy since the image of God was, for St. Gregory, totally immaterial and rational. Some scholars, Harold Cherniss, for example, think that in trying to combine Christianity and Platonism, St. Gregory came very close to intellectual dishonesty:

> at the end it seems that, but for some few orthodox dogmas which he could not circumvent, Gregory has merely applied Christian names to Plato's doctrine and called it Christian

theology. These few dogmas, however, made of his writings a sorry spectacle. He has so far accepted and insisted upon the pure immateriality of the world of the resurrection that it is impossible for him to explain a physical resurrection, while to accept the latter on faith means the damnation of all his previous argument. But he does accept the dogma and even tries to account for it, although his account comes tottering to the gulf of complete denial. He has up to this point argued so successfully that his reader must reject either the entire argument or the absurdly unconnected conclusion. . . . He would be orthodox at any cost of intellectual integrity.[2]

Gerhard Ladner takes a somewhat more sympathetic view but acknowledges the problem:

If the resurrection belongs to the restoration of all things to their primitive integrity, why then should man again become a spiritual-corporeal composite? For, did not God originally create man in His image which is spiritual. . . .? There remains here, nevertheless, a certain lack of clarity or explicitness in the Bishop of Nyssa's doctrine which, perhaps explains in part the serious charges against Gregory's consistency raised by H. Cherniss. . . . The coherence of Gregory's whole anthropology does indeed hinge on the question whether or not he believed that it could have been meaningful for man, the spiritual image of God, to have a body even without sin.[3]

Ladner goes on to offer a solution by referring to the luminous garments which St. Gregory mentioned in his writings but did not very clearly explain. According to Ladner, the soul will be resurrected in a luminous garment which could be a kind of body similar to the angels' but without the mortality or sexuality of animals. This resurrectional body or luminous garment, is what Adam and Eve possessed after the second creation but before the fall and their reception of the garments of skin. They were bodily creatures having a certain light materiality with senses and an angelic type of reproduction. Their being clothed with gross animality, the garments of skin, was the result of the fall since in their luminous, light garments, Adam and Eve were immortal and had their beings properly ordered with the rational image controlling the irrational, but not yet passionate, material elements. With the garments of skin came powerful, foreign forces (the passions) which upset the balance and order, and instead of allowing the rational element (the image) to rule from top down, the animal passions ruled from the bottom up.

Jean Daniélou comes to a similar conclusion:

> This is not to say that every "body" is foreign to this [human] "nature." It is quite certain that Gregory sometimes assimilates it to the angels' nature. . . . But, on the other hand, we do find in his writings other expressions that imply that he accepted a bodily state, different from the one we know now, but nonetheless real. These are the "luminous tunics" . . . of which he sometimes speaks: "When each of us sees the tunics of skin that envelop our nature and those delicate leaves with which we have been clothed after having put off our former luminous clothes. . . ." Elsewhere, he speaks of the Father who restores to the prodigal son "his tunic, but though not another tunic, but rather the first one he had, the one he lost after being disobedient. . . ." It is this "tunic of incorruption" that Christ gives to the newly baptized person. . . . Thus, in the Treatise on the Soul and the Resurrection, Gregory speaks of the "bodily clothing . . . dissolved by death and which is woven together again, not in this thick nature . . . but in a light and airy manner.[4]

Not all the interpreters of St. Gregory's thought are willing to let him get out of his Platonic-Christian dilemma so easily. He contributed to his own problem because he was not always clear in his writings. Cherniss, as we have seen, is one of his most severe critics, but even Ladner must admit that his attempt at reconciliation is inadequate, and St. Gregory may in fact have been confused and contradictory in his own mind:

It is not my intention. . . . to smooth out all the difficulties of Gregory of Nyssa's anthropological thought. . . . Yet, there remains in Gregory of Nyssa's thinking, I would not say, a contradiction, but a tension which it seems to me, is also a part of his greatness. It is in short, the tension between the Gregorian, the Cappadocian, and generally, the Platonizing form of Greek Christian spirituality and the ineluctable materiality of the physical world which included non-human nature.[5]

Another problem which St. Gregory left unsolved was the relation of sin and death. According to Scripture, death was not a feature of the creation before sin. How is it, then, that animal life is naturally mortal? For it was with this kind of life that Adam and Eve were clothed and thus became mortal just by taking on animality. Was death introduced into the animal world by some other agency, angelic sin perhaps? Are animals naturally mortal? If so, then, death could not have come by sin, and it is natural to the creation, being only an instrument of man's purification after the fall and not the direct result of his disobedience. This problem is not adequately solved even by Ladner's interpretation because Adam and Eve did not become mortal until they received the garments of skin.

After all is said and done, the fundamental Platonic distinction between the ideal and material strongly shows through in all of St. Gregory's works. If on the purely denotational level of his words and concepts he can be saved from the charge of having contempt for the material creation, on the level of the connotation of his words, their feel, it is difficult not to conclude that in his mind sin is associated with matter, body, sex, etc. If these things are not sinful in themselves, then they are at least nasty and to be avoided by the serious Christian. On the other hand, the feel of his words associates goodness and holiness with spiritual, non-material, rational things. Whether St. Gregory tried to adapt his Platonism to his Christianity or vice versa, the aftertaste of pagan philosophy is too strong to use St. Gregory's so-called system as a basis for a satisfying Christian anthropology. Perhaps the saving grace in all this is his oft-stated acknowledgement that his statements were his ideas, speculations, and musings on the subject. He did not take his doctrines with ultimate seriousness, and so we too are free to say "yes, but."

## ICONOGRAPHY

In her iconography, the Church portrays by material means the transfigured world to come, the Kingdom of God. The implication of this doctrine is that the things of this world that are not to be part of the Kingdom are not portrayed or are portrayed in some subservient, conquered position. All things are shown in a transformed way indicating how they will be then and not how they are now. There are exceptions to this rule that require special explanations, such as the old man-devil in the Nativity or Judas in the Mystical Supper, but in general it holds. An icon is by definition a material thing: its physical elements are used by a Christian artist to portray a level of being that we can only glimpse and get a whiff of now. But because presently existing material elements are capable of prefiguring this eschatological reality, we know that there is a connection between this artistic material and the world to come. There is no radical disconnection, no rejection of the now for the then, but a transformation of things and people. In other words, what we know of this present world can be changed and projected into the Kingdom; it can be sanctified and transfigured because it is basically good and capable of carrying the divine energies.

If we want to get an idea of what this transfiguration will be like, we have at least three sources to study: 1) Christ's resurrectional appearances, 2) scriptural statements about the Kingdom, and 3) iconography. What do we see in these sources? We see a world at once radically different from our own and at the same time very similar. We see Christ appearing in rooms through locked doors, being recognized as a man, having people touch him, eating fish, etc.: similar yet different. In the Beatitudes, we hear about a world where the values on which our present world runs are turned upside down and where the meek and not the rich and powerful shall inherit the earth: similar but different. In icons, we see colors, shapes, lines buildings, people, and things, but not quite the way they appear to us now: similar but different. Both these elements, the similar and the different, continuity and change, need to be stressed. The only things we know now that have no place in our three sources are death and those elements which derive their power from it, such as tyranny, which can only exist where the ultimate threat of death is feared. The Church is telling us that the material world, both by its sanctification in the making of icons themselves and by its portrayal in a transfigured way in them, can be projected into the Kingdom. It is not ultimately alien to God or an afterthought of creation, a type of second class creation. In the hierarchical order of creation, matter is on a lower level, so to speak, but not because it is on the lower side of the spirit/matter divide but because it is on the lower side of the life/non-life divide. Since matter can be used in the service of God, it is part of the original plan of creation; it is theophoric – God-bearing – and therefore projectable into the Kingdom.

What can iconography tell us about man as part of the fallen and transfigured creation? The first thing to notice about humans portrayed in icons is that they look like humans as we know them. They can never be confused with any other creature. They are of course different in their look: physical proportions are different, one size does not fit all, features of youth and old age are combined, but still men and women are recognizable as humans. And how are they recognized: – in their bodies just as they are recognized now. How else would they be recognized? They are also recognizable in their bodies as men and women; sexual distinctions are not suppressed in icons – transformed, yes, but not suppressed. Even such gender-based distinctions and relations as mother, father, husband, wife, family, conception (the icon of the Conception of the Theotokos and John the Baptist), and nursing[6] are shown. By implication, it must be assumed that these are transformable in some way so as to have a place in the Kingdom.

Now we know that in the Kingdom there will be no marriage or giving in marriage, but we know also from the Church's teaching that there is something of the Kingdom in Christian marriage, and it too is projectable into that new world to come. The male-female distinction cannot be an afterthought,but is essentially identified with man's creation in the image of God. What we learn from the Genesis story as filtered down through Holy Tradition is that man is and was created in the image of God. Therefore, whatever we call and show as essentially human is in the image of God. The image cannot be identified with just a part of that composite entity called a human being. If we show a man or a woman in an icon with a transfigured body similar to but different from what we know now, we are implying that a body, whatever its actual state in the Kingdom, is part of man and so a part of the image of God.

The exact make-up of the image of God in man cannot be described or localized; it is ultimately a mystery as are all the dogmas of the faith. In fact, it is better not to speak of the "image of God in man" as though man were the larger entity containing something called an image of God. We should rather say "man as the image of God." Here the emphasis is rightly put on man first as a created, whole being who at the same time is made entirely in the image of God. We might be able to say that this or that aspect of man seems to be more or less Godlike; that is our speculation, but we cannot exclude anything from the scope of the image if we claim that man as a whole, and not some part of him, is in the image. Man's materiality and sexuality, then, must figure in the original plan of God and must be incorporated into the concept of the image. They are not the result of sin, to be discarded after the period of tutelage is over. Iconography supports the principle of "similar but different," continuity with change. The redemption of man is, therefore, not a matter of surgery, cutting away something alien and super-added at an earlier time, but a matter of redressing a balance, reordering of elements put out of balance by the sin and death which caused dislocations throughout man's whole being.

## CRITIQUE OF ST. GREGORY'S
## POSITION IN THE LIGHT
## OF ICONOGRAPHY

Let us begin with St. Gregory's most basic doctrine about man, the "two creations" theory: the first creation of man in the non-material, rational image of God, and the second of Adam and Eve as material, sexual, and mortal. Of course, behind this idea is the Platonic distinction between ideal and material reality, the "really real" being spiritual and the diminished reality being material. We cannot accept this interpretation of the creation or of the image because it does not define real humanity as having a material dimension from the beginning. In fact, all the problems in St. Gregory's anthropology come directly from his attempt to maintain this principle and to adapt it to the Christian faith. If anyone talks about the Christian doctrine of man while holding such a philosophical position, he is doomed to do violence to one or the other position. They both cannot be held with integrity. There cannot, therefore, be two creations, ideal and material whereby the image of God is identified with only the spiritual, rational part. From the beginning, materiality must figure in God's plan for the "really real" man.

The non-sexual character of St. Gregory's ideal man in the image of God cannot be accepted either. As far as the exegesis of Genesis 1:27 is concerned, there is no reason, except that of his pre-existing Platonic philosophy, to break up the verse, which otherwise forms a natural unit, in order to differentiate the asexual man in the image of God from the sexual Adam and Eve in their garments of skin. The male/female distinction too must be seen as belonging to the image and part of God's original and eschatological plan.

A corollary to his view of man's sexual nature is St. Gregory's notion of marriage and the role of virginity. Since sexuality and marriage are grounded in the gross animality of the garments of skin, it is possible to use them for good only if the rational part of man dominates and controls the passionate parts. It is even necessary for some to marry in order for man to fulfill himself in history and not to become extinct, but because the original man in the image of God was not and will not be sexually differentiated, it is better, for those really dedicated to the spiritual life, to abstain from marriage and remain virgins. For those truly seeking God, the implication of St. Gregory's words is quite clear:

> Marriage, then, is the last stage of our separation from the life that was led in Paradise; marriage, therefore, . . . is the first thing to be left; it is the first station as it were of our departure to Christ.[7]

Jean Daniélou summarizes St. Gregory's position as follows:

> In his treatise, Gregory enumerates all the advantages of virginity. . . . But what is the basic principle of them all is that virginity is man's return to his true nature and that it is therefore an anticipation of the resurrection at the same time as a return to the state of paradise. . . . Virginity is therefore not a necessary means of salvation but on the one hand is a witness to the true human condition and has a prophetic value; on the other, virginity creates better conditions for sanctification.[8]

Whatever is the place of virginity in the Church, and there is certainly a place for it – is it not preferable to talk of monasticism since it is a broader term and does not concentrate so much on sex? – St. Gregory's thought lacks a development of virginity's counterpart, Christian marriage. Little if anything is said about this means of transforming life into the Kingdom. St. Gregory distinguished marriage and virginity when in fact he should have made a three-fold division: "natural" marriage, Christian marriage, and consecrated virginity. He thus contributed to perpetuating the imbalance in the Church's thinking on this matter.

St. Gregory's dynamic of salvation for men and women in their garments of skin is to struggle by ascetical and spiritual efforts to maintain the dominion of the rational element over the irrational, passionate parts of their makeup. The subjugation of the animal passions and their transformation into virtues goes on as long as the rational image is clothed in the garments of skin. But with death, the garments are lost, men are no longer swept to and fro by the gross animality of earthly existence, and the immaterial image takes a giant step forward towards its restoration.

We have here the surgical model of salvation. The ordering of the image over the body and of the mind over matter is, accordingly, only an earthly activity to be carried on until the garments of skin can be gotten rid of. The reordering of all the elements and the maintenance of the balance, however, are activities to be projected into the Kingdom. What will be lost or destroyed, the thing which now hinders our different faculties from working as they should, is not materiality itself but rather the environment, which is inside of us too. This environment is dominated by the alien power of death. When it is destroyed, and its power is removed from us and the creation, man in the image of God will naturally manifest himself as God-bearing, and all of his parts will work together in the proper order.

## CONCLUSION

Do we have a more satisfactory doctrine if we follow Ladner's and Daniélou's interpretation of St. Gregory whereby they posit a three-fold creation involving: 1) ideal, rational creation; 2) material, gendered creation but in light, airy, and luminous garments; and 3) fall into gross, sexual, mortal animality? This position is certainly an improvement from the point of view of the criticisms made so far because it admits the possibility of being material, of having a body, and of being male and female before the fall. These things, therefore, are not the result of sin, but, at the same time, the Platonic dichotomy is not overcome, and they are not part of the original immaterial and rational image. The starting point must be that these elements were introduced as parts of man in the image of God from the beginning. Since they leave their traces in the Kingdom, they must have their roots in paradise. Though this interpretation sounds good, Ladner and Daniélou admit that it is not certain that St. Gregory would himself have accepted it. He may have been more rigorist in his Platonism than they would like to make him out.

St. Gregory is a classical example of a Christian thinker's attempt to combine a philosophical tradition with Christian doctrine. In this case, Platonic philosophy antedates Christianity by several hundred years. It has its own structure and does not need to adapt itself to Christian models to maintain its integrity. Christianity also does not need any particular philosophy from outside itself to proclaim a consistent message. In St. Gregory, as in other Christian philosopher-theologians, we see the great danger of trying to knit together two visions of the world which can basically do without each other. Although it is not wrong to attempt to marry the two, we should not expect great results. After all, the Biblical vision of man, and not the Platonic vision, should be at the base of all Christian anthropology. Icons are in clear continuity with the Biblical vision.

The world view portrayed in icons is the Church's view of a metarational mystery, our metahistorical destiny in the Kingdom. The deathbound categories of this world and its philosophies are not easily integrated into that mystery. By comparing St. Gregory's speculation on man as the image of God with the Church's vision of that same reality, we have a good model for evaluating all Christian thinkers: we must reflect theological discourse off the mirror of the Church's experience of the metarational mystery. Priority should always be given to lived experience over any constructed system of thought. We have here a very Orthodox principle: cataphatic discourse takes us only so far into the mystery, but apophatic silence before the mystery, in this case shown in icons, takes us to the heart, to the experience of the Kingdom.

# NOTES

1 Gregory of Nyssa, "On the Soul and the Resurrection," *Nicene and Post-Nicene Fathers* V, Eerdmans, 1979, p. 465.

2 Harold F. Cherniss, *The Platonism of Gregory of Nyssa*, New York, Lenox Hill Publishing, 1971, pp. 62-63.

3 Gerhard Ladner, "The Anthropology of Gregory of Nyssa," *Dumbarton Oaks Papers* 12, Cambridge, Mass., Harvard, 1958, p. 87.

4 Jean Daniélou, *Platonisme et théologie mystique: Doctrine spirituelle de saint Grégoire de Nysse*, Paris, Aubier: Editions Montaigne, 1944, p. 57.

5 Ladner, pp. 94-95.

6 John Taylor, *Icon Painting*, New York, Mayflower Books, Inc., 1959, p. 50.

7 Gregory of Nyssa, "On Virginity" 12, *Nicene and Post-Nicene Fathers* V, p. 358.

8 Daniélou, pp. 52-53.

# BIBLIOGRAPHY

*Acts of the Moscow Council of 1666-67.* The Holy Synod of the Russian Church, 1893.

Alexander, J. P., "The Iconoclastic Council of St. Sophia (815) and Its Definition (Horos)," *Dumbarton Oaks Papers* 7, 1953.

Anastos, M. "The Argument for Iconoclasm as Presented by the Iconoclastic Council of 754," in *Late Classical and Medieval Studies in Honor of A. M. Friend, Jr.* Princeton: 1954.

*The Ante-Nicene Fathers.* 3 vols. Grand Rapids, Mich.: Eerdmans Publishing, 1979-80.

Ariès, Philippe. *The Hour of Our Death* New York: Knopf, 1981.

Barrois, George A. *The Face of Christ in the Old Testament.* Crestwood, N.Y.: St. Vladimir's Seminary Press, 1974.

Bartlet, C. *Church-Life and Church-Order during the First Four Centuries.* Oxford: Blackwell, 1934.

Behr-Sigel, E. "La sophiologie du Père S. Boulgakov," *Le messager orthodoxe*, 57:I (1972): pp. 21-48.

Bernard, Charles. "L'activité symbolique," *Théologie symbolique.* Paris: Téqui, 1978.

Bettenson, Henry. *The Early Christian Fathers.* London: Oxford University Press, 1963.

Bœspflug, François. *Dieu dans l'art.* Paris: Cerf, 1984.

Bossuet, *Culte des Images*, I, *Œuvres complètes*, Bloud et Barral, III, *Controverse*, cited from *Dictionnaire de Théologie Catholique*, 7, 1. Paris: Librairie Letouzey et Ané, 1927.

Bovini, G. I *Sarcofagi paleocristiani della Spagna.* Rome: The Pontifical Institute of Christian Archaeology, 1954.

Bréhier, Louis. *L'Art chrétien: son développement iconographique des origines à nos jours.* Paris: 1918.

Bulgakov, S. *The Clergy Manual.* (in Russian) Kiev: 1913.

Canévet, Mariette. "Grégoire de Nysse," *Dictionnaire de Spiritualité*, VI. Paris: Beauchesne, 1967.

*The Canons and Decrees of the Council of Trent.* T. Buckley, tr. London: Routledge, 1851.

Cherniss, Harold F. *The Platonism of Gregory of Nyssa.* New York: Lenox Hill Publishing, 1971.

*The Code of Canon Law: A Text and Commentary.* J. Coriden et al, eds. London: Chapman, 1984.

"Commentary on Daniel," *PG*, 81: 1321-25.

*The Complete Collection of the Decisions of the Department of the Or-*

*thodox Confession.* Vol. 2. (in Russian)

Connolly, H. *Didascalia Apostolorum.* Oxford: The Clarendon Press, 1929.

Cormack, Robin. "Painting after Iconoclasm." In *Iconoclasm: 9th Spring Symposium on Byzantine Studies,* pp. 142-163. Birmingham, U.K.: Birmingham Centre for Byzantine Studies, Univ. of Birmingham, 1977

Cornell, T. and J. Matthews. *Atlas du monde romain.* Paris: Fernand Nathan, 1984.

Daniélou, Jean. *Platonisme et théologie mystique: Doctrine spirituelle de saint Grégoire de Nysse* Paris: Aubier: Editions Montaigne, 1944.

"De l'Invocation de la Vénération et des Reliques, des Saints et des Saintes Images." *Le Saint Concile de Trente,* 2, Session 25. M. L'Abbé Dassance, trans. Paris: 1842.

Diadochus of Photice. *Œuvres spirituelles, Sources chrétiennes, 5.* E. des Places, trans. Paris: Cerf, 1966.

*Dictionnaire d'Archéologie chrétienne et de Liturgie.* Paris: Librairie Letouzey et Ané, 1920.

*Dictionnaire de Théologie Catholique*

*Dictionnaire des conciles.* M. Minge, ed. Paris: 1847.

Didron, M. *Christian Iconography.* I. E. J. Millington, trans. London: 1851.

Dionysius of Fourna. *The "Painter's Manual" of Dionysius of Fourna.* Paul Hetherington, trans. London: Roebuck Press, 1978. Reprint. Redondo Beach, Calif.: Oakwood Publications, 1989.

Drobot, Georges. *Icône de la Nativity.* Spiritualité orientale, 15. Abbaye de Bellefontaine, 1975.

Duchesne, E. *Le Stoglav ou les Cent chapitres: Recueil des Décisions de l'Assemblée Ecclésiastique de Moscou, 1551, Bibliothèque de l'Institut Français de Petrograd, 5. Librairie Ancienne.* Honoré Champion, ed. Paris: 1920.

*Euchologe ou rituel de l'Eglise orthodoxe.* Archimandrite Alexandre Nilidow and Natoine Nivière, trans. Paix: Le Bousquet d'Orb, France, 1979. Slavonic version ed. by Trebnik. Moscow: Holy Synod of the Russian Orthodox Church, 1911.

*Evangiles avec Peintures Byzantines du XIe Siècle, 1 and 2, Reproduction des 361 Miniatures du Manuscrit grec 74 de la Bibliothèque Nationale.* H. Omont, ed. Imprimerie Berthaud Frères, 1908.

Evdokimov, Paul. *The Art of the Icon: A Theology of Beauty.* Redondo Beach, Calif.: Oakwood Publications, 1990.

*The Festal Menaion.* Mother Mary and Archimandrite Kallistos Ware, trans. London: Faber and Faber, 1969.

*Les fresques de Pompéi.* Paris: Editions Atlas, 1983.

Galavaris, George. *The Illustrations of the Liturgical Homilies of Gregory Nazianzus.* Princeton, N.J.: Princeton Univ. Press, 1969.

Galey, John. *Sinai and the Monastery of St. Catherine*. Garden City, N.Y.: Doubleday, 1980.

Gaudemet, J., "Le concile d'Elvire," Dictionnaire d'Histoire de de Géographie Ecclésiastique, 15, 1963.

Gerstinger, Hans. "Uber Herkunft und Entwicklung der Anthropomorphen Byzantinisch-Slavischen Trinitats-darstellungen des Sogenannten Synthronoi-und Paternitas-(Otéchestow) Typus." *Festschrift W. Sas-Zaloziecky zum 60 Gerburtstag, Akademische Druck-U*, pp. 79 ff. Graz: Verlagsanstalt, 1956.

Gerstinger, Hans. *Die Griechische Buchmalerei*. Vienna: 1926.

Gouillard, J. "Grégoire II et l'Iconoclasme," *Travaux et Mémoires*, Centre de Recherche d'histoire et civilisation byzantines, III, Paris, 1968.

——————— "Le Synodikon de l'Orthodoxie: Edition et Textes," *Travaux et Mémoires*, 2. Paris: Centre de Recherche d'histoire et civilisation byzantines, 1967.

Grabar, André. *Byzantine Painting*. New York: Rizzoli, 1979.

——————— *Christian Iconography: A Study of Its Origins*. Princeton, N. J.: Princeton Univ. Press, 1968.

——————— *Early Christian Art: From the Rise of Christiantiy to the Death of Theodosius* New York: Odyssey Press, 1968.

——————— *L'iconoclasme byzantin*. Paris: Flammarion, 1984.

Grant, Michael. *The Art and Life of Pompeii and Herculaneum*. New York: New Week Books, 1979.

Gregory Nazianzen. "The Second Theological Oration," *Oration XXVIII. The Nicene and Post-Nicene Fathers*, 7. Grand Rapids, Mich.: Eerdmans Publishing, 1979.

Gregory of Nyssa. "On the Making of Man." *The Nicene and Post-Nicene Fathers*, 5. Grand Rapids, Mich.: Eerdmans Publishing, 1979.

——————— "On the Soul and the Resurrection." *The Nicene and Post-Nicene Fathers 5*. Grand Rapids, Mich.: Eerdmans Publishing, 1979.

——————— "On Virginity," 12. *The Nicene and Post-Nicene Fathers 5*. Grand Rapids, Mich.: Eerdmans Publishing, 1979.

——————— *From Glory to Glory: Texts from Gregory of Nyssa's Mystical Writings*. Jean Daniélou, ed. Crestwood, N. Y.: St. Vladimir's Seminary Press, 1979.

Gregory Palamas, "Homily on the Presentation of the Holy Virgin in the Temple." *Sem. Kond. VII*.

Grumel, V. "Images (Culte Des)" *Dictionnaire de Théologie Catholique, 7, 1*. Paris: Librairie Letouzey et Ané, 1927.

——————— "L'Iconologie de Saint Germain de Constantinople," *Echos d'Orient*, 21 (1922): pp. 165-75.

Harden, J. M. *The Ethiopic Didascalia, XXI*. New York: Society for Promoting Christian Knowledge, 1920,

Hautecoeur, L. "Le Concile de Trente et l'art," *Il Concilio di Trento e la ariforma tridentina, Atti del Convegno storico internazionale*

(September 1965).

Hefele, C. J. *A History of the Councils of the Church, 626-787*. Wm. R. Clark, trans. Edinburgh: T. T. Clark, 1896.

—————— *Histoire des Conciles* III-2, Paris.

Heimann, Adelheid. "L'Iconographie de la Trinité." *L'Art chrétien*, I (October, 1934): p. 140.

Hippolytus of Rome. The Apostolic Tradition, II, 11. Gregory Dix, ed., New York: The Macmillan Company, 1937.

Hopko, Thomas. *The Orthodox Faith*. Vol. I, *Doctrine*. New York: The Department of Religious Education: The Orthodox Church in America, 1981.

Horner, G. *The Statues of the Apostles or Canones Ecclesiastici*, "The Translation of the Arabic Text," 27: "Concerning the new persons . . . and the occupations which it is proper they should give up . . . ".

—————— *The Statues of the Apostles or Canones Ecclesiastici*, "Translation of the Saidic Text," 41: "Concerning the Occupations and the Crafts." London: 1904.

Hough, James. *History of Christianity in India*, vol. II. R. London: B. Seeley and W. Burnside, 1839.

Ignatius of Antioch. "Epistle to Polycarp, III." *The Ante-Nicene Fathers*, Vol. 1. Grand Rapids, Mich.: Eerdmans Publishing, 1979.

Irenæus of Lyons. "Against Heresies," I. *Ante-Nicene Fathers*, Vol. 1. Grand Rapids, Mich.: Eerdmans Publishing, 1979.

John Chrysostom. *On St. John*, PG 59.

—————— *On the Divine Images*. David Anderson, trans. Crestwood, N.Y.: St. Vladimir's Seminary Press, 1980.

—————— *Sur l'incompréhensibilité de Dieu. Sources Chrétiennes,* 28bis. Paris: Cerf.

John of Thessolonica. "Mansii," XIII, col. 101. Cited from Grumel, V. "Images (Culte Des)," *Dictionnaire de Théologie Catholique*, 7, 1. Paris: Librairie Letouzey et Ané, 1927: p. 838.

Jugie, M. "Constantinople (IVe Concile de)," *Dictionnaire de Théologique Catholique, III*, pp. 1297 ff. Paris: Librairie Letouzey et Ané, 1908.

Justin Martyr. "Dialogue with Trypho," *Ante-Nicene Fathers, I.* Grand Rapids, Mich.: Eerdmans Publishing, 1979.

Kalokyris, Constantine. *The Byzantine Wall-Paintings of Crete*. New York: Red Dust 1973.

—————— *The Essence of Orthodox Iconography*. Brookline, Mass.: Holy Cross School of Theology, Hellenic College, 1971.

Kantorowicz, Ernst. "The Quinity of Winchester," *The Art Bulletin*, 29.1, (March 1947): pp. 73-85.

Kazakova, N. A. and Ia. S. Lourié. *The Heretical, Antifeudal Movements in Russia from the 14th century to the Beginning of the 16th Century*. (in Russian), Moscow-Leningrad: 1955.

Kelly, J.N.D. *Early Christian Doctrine*. London: Adam and Charles

Black, 1975.

Klauser, Theodor. "Studien zur Entstehungsgeschicte der Christlichen Kunst," III. *Jahrbuch für Antike und Christentum,* Jahrgang 3 (1960).

Kraeling, C. *The Christian Building, The Excavations at Dura-Europos: The Christian Building,* Final Report VIII-2. New Haven: Dura-Europos Publications, 1967.

Ladner, Gerhard, "The Anthropology of Gregory of Nyssa," *Dumbarton Oaks Papers 12.* Cambridge, Mass.: Harvard Univ. Press, 1958.

Laeuchli, S. Power and Sexuality: *The Emergence of Canon Law at the Synod of Elvira.* Philadelphia: Temple University Press, 1972.

Lanne, E. "Rome et les saintes images," *Irénikon* 2, 1986.

Larchet, Jean-Claude. *Thérapeutique des maladies spirituelles.* Paris: Les Editions de l'Ancre, 1991.

Lassus, Jean. *The Early Christian and Byzantine World.* London: Paul Hamlyn, 1967.

Le Bachelet. "Alexandre VIII," Dictionnaire de Théologie Catholique 1-1.

Lebeau, Paul. *Aux origines de l'art chrétien.* Brussels: Lumen Vitae, 1987.

Leclercq, Henri, "Images (Culte et Querelle des)," *Dictionnaire d'Archéologie chrétienne et de Liturgie,* 7, 1, pp. 273 ff. Paris: Librairie Letouzey et Ané, 1920.

Leroquais, V. *Le Bréviaire de Philippe le Bon.* Bruxelles: 1927.

Leys, Roger. *L'Image de Dieu chez saint Grégoire de Nysse.* Paris: Desclée de Brouwer, 1951.

*Livres des lettres.* Tiflis: 1901 in Sirarpie der Nersessian, "Une Apologie des Images du 7e siècle," *Byzantion* XVII, 1944-45.

Lossky, Vladimir. *The Vision of God.* Clayton, Wisc.: The Faith Press, 1963.

Lowrie, Walter. *Art in the Early Church.* New York: W. W. Norton, 1969.

Mâle, Emile. *The Religious Art in France: The Twelfth Century.* Princeton, N.J.: Princeton University Press, 1978.

Mango, C. *The Art of the Byzantine Empire 312-1453: Sources and Documents.* Toronto: University of Toronto Press, 1986,.

Martin, John. *The Illustration of the Heavenly Ladder of St. John Climacus.* Princeton, N.J.: Princeton Univ. Press, 1954.

Meyendorff, John. "L'iconographie de la Sagesse divine dans la tradition byzantine." *Byzantine Hesychasm: Historical, Theological and Social Problems,* pp. 259-277. London: Variorum Reprints, 1974.

Miquel, Pierre. "Culte des Images," *Dictionnaire de Spiritualité, Fas. XLVIII-XLIX,* pp. 1515-16. Paris: Beauchesne, 1970.

Nau. *La version syriaque de l'Octateuque de Clément II,* II,1. Reedited by Pio Ciprotti. Paris: Lethielleux, 1967.

Nersessian, Sirarpie der. "Une Apologie des Images du 7e siècle,"

*Byzantion* XVII, 1944-45.

Nersessian, Vrej. *The Tondrakian Movement*. Allison Park, Penn.: Pickwick Publications, 1987.

Ostrogorsky, Georg. "Les Décisions du 'Stoglav' Concernant la Peinture d'Images et les Principes de l'Iconographie Byzantine," *Byzanz und Die Welt Der Slawen*. Darmstadt: Wissenschaftliche Buchgesellschaft, 1974.

Ouspensky, Léonide and Vladimir Lossky. *The Meaning of Icons*. Bern: URS Graf Verlag, 1952. Reprint. Boston: Boston Book and Art Shop, 1969.

————— *The Meaning of Icons*. Rev. ed. Crestwood, N.Y.: St. Vladimir's Seminary Press, 1982.

Ouspensky, Léonide. "Quelques considérations au sujet de l'iconographie de la Pentecôte," *Messager de l'Exarchat du patriarcat russe*, (1960): pp.33-34.

————— *La Théologie de l'icône dans l'Eglise orthodoxe*. Paris: Cerf, 1980.

————— *The Theology of the Icon*. Crestwood, N.Y.: St. Vladimir's Seminary Press, 1978.

Ozoline, Nicolas. "La doctrine boulgakovienne de la 'descriptibilité' de Dieu à la lumière de la théologie orthodoxe de l'icône," *Le messager orthodoxe*, 98 (1985): pp. 111-129.

Papadopoulos, S. A.. "Essai d'"interprétation du Thème iconographique de la Paternité dans l'Art Byzantin," *Cahiers Archéologiques*, 18 (1968): pp. 134 ff.

*Patriologia Orientalis* XXXI, 2, Les canons d'Hippolyte, Paris: René-Georges Coquin, 1966.

*Le Pentecostaire*. Tomes.1–2. Père Denis Guillaume, trans. Rome: Collège de Rome, 1978.

Pius XII (Pope). "Mediator Dei," *The Papal Encyclicals 1939-1958*. Raleigh, N. C.: McGrath Publishing, 1981.

*Les psaumes: prières de l'Eglise*. Père Placide Deseille, trans. Paris: YMCA-Press, 1979.

Réau, Louis. *Iconographie de l'art chrétien: II, Iconographie de la Bible: I, Ancien Testament*. Presses Universitaires de France, 1956.

Rice, David Talbot. *Art of the Byzantine Era*. London: Thames and Hudson, 1963.

Sahas, D. *Icon and Logos: Sources in Eighth century Iconoclasm*. Toronto: University of Toronto, 1986

"The Second Theological Oration, Oration XXVIII, ch. III." The Nicene and Post-Nicene Fathers, 7. Grand Rapids, Mich.: Eerdmans Publishing, 1979.

Sendler, Egon. *The Icon: Image of the Invisible*. Redondo Beach, Calif.: Oakwood Publications, 1988.

Sethad. *Bibliotheca graeca mediiaevi* Vol. 3. Venice: 1872.

*The Seven Ecumenical Councils*. Henry Percival, ed. *The Nicene and Post-Nicene Fathers,* 14. Grand Rapids, Mich Eerdmans Publishing, 1979.

Sherrard, Philip. *Athos the Holy Mountain.* Woodstock, N.Y.: Overlook Press, 1982.

Spiridon, Archimandrite. *Mes missions en Sibérie.* Paris: Cerf, 1968.

Taylor, John. *Icon Painting.* New York: Mayflower Books, 1959.

———— *Icon Paintings.* New York: Mayflower Books, 1979.

Tertullian. *Adversus Praxean. The Ante-Nicene Fathers,* 3. Grand Rapids, Mich.: Eerdmans Publishing, 1980.

Thaliath, J. "The Synod of Diamper," *Orient Christiana Analecta,* 152. Rome: 1958.

Theodore the Studite. *On the Holy Icons.* Catherine P. Roth, trans. Crestwood, N.Y.: St. Vladimir's Seminary Press, 1981.

Theodoret of Cyrrhus. "Commentary on Daniel." *PG,* 81: 1321-25.

Thunberg, L.. "Early Christian Interpretations of the Three Angels in Gen. 18," *Studia Patristica, VII ("Texte und Untersuchungen", 92),* pp. 560-70. Berlin: 1966.

*Le Triode de Carême,* tomes 1–3. P. Denis Guillaume, trans., Rome: Collège Grec de Rome, 1978.

Vasileios, Archimandrite. *Hymn of Entry.* Crestwood, N.Y.: St. Vladimir's Seminary Press, 1984.

*Vision 12: Œuvres spirituelles.* E. des Places, trans. *Sources chrétiennes,* 5 (1966)

Von Schonborn, Christoph. *L'icône du Christ: fondements théologiques.* Fribourg, Switzerland: Editions Universitaires, 1976.

Watler, Christopher. "'La Pentecôte', L'iconographie des conciles dans la tradition byzantine." *Archives de l'Orient Chrétien,* 13 (1970): pp. 190-214.

Yanagi, Munemoto, et al. *Byzantium.* Secaucus, N.J.: Chartwell Books, 1978.

# SOURCES OF ILLUSTRATIONS

Evangiles avec Peintures Byzantines du XIe Siècle
　　*figure 11.*
Galey, John, Sinai and the Monastery of St. Catherine
　　*figures 1, 2, 15, and 16.*
Gerstinger, Hans, "Uber Herkunft . . . "
　　*figures 18, 19, and 20.*
——— Die Griechische Buchmalerei
　　*figure 20.*
Grabar, André, Christian Iconography
　　*figure 20.*
——— Byzantine Painting
　　*figure 12.*
——— Early Christian Art
　　*figure 3.*
Kalokyris, Donstantin, The Byzantine Wall-Paintings of Crete
　　*figure 29.*
Kantorowicz, Ernst, "The Quinity of Winchester,"
　　*figures 22, 23, 24, 25, 26, and 27.*
Lassus, Jean, The Early Christian and Byzantine World
　　*figure 28.*
Martin, John, The Illustration of the Heavenly Ladder of St. John
　　Climacus
　　*figure 17.*
Rice, David Talbot, Art of the Byzantine Era
　　*figure 5.*

# COLOPHON

Written by Fr. Stephen Bigham

Published by Philip Tamoush
Oakwood Publications
Torrance, CA

Typeset in *ITC Berkeley Oldstyle*
with *Sophia*
running heads by
George Bedrin
οιδα
Grand Isle, VT
&
Nicholas Turnbull
*Atelier Analgoion*
Montréal, QC
Proofreader: Michael Carney

Thanks to Hieromonk Serge
&
Iconographer Tom Doolan
for their editorial comments.